ENDORSEMENTS FOR *SEASONS OF A LEADER'S LIFE*

FROM A LEARNER—

As an aspiring new leader, I am always looking for tools to help me steward my leadership development. This book has important insights God has used to shape both my character and leadership skills. Dr. Iorg provides insight to experienced leaders, while also remaining accessible to beginning leaders like me. It also helps me to think about leaving my legacy, starting now, and working toward that lifelong goal.

James Westbrook, seminary student and an emerging leader

FROM A LEADER—

The season of leading will keep you up at night and turn your hair gray! But it will also fill your heart and invigorate your soul. Active leadership is both exhilarating and exhausting. Nevertheless, it's our God-given task. We're in the game, not on the bench. We are in the race, not coaching or cheering. There's nothing better than leading, and having people follow! So rise up, dream big, and implement the vision God gives you. In these pages, Dr. Iorg will inspire and encourage you as a leader. As you lead, you will feel God's pleasure and marvel at His impact through you. So read these pages, run His race, and lead for the joy of Jesus!

Gregg Matte, Senior Pastor, First Baptist Church,
Houston, Texas

FROM A LEGACY-LEAVER—

As a young pastor, someone told me, "Don't fizzle at the finish." Through the years, I've observed some leaders who finished well, some poorly, and some who failed or quit. Dr. Iorg writes about leaving a legacy—the ultimate goal of every leader! Follow his counsel and you will be able to say with Paul that you "finished the race" God has given you to complete. Leaders lead to the end, leaving a legacy for coming generations.

Jim Henry, Pastor Emeritus, First Baptist Church,
Orlando, Florida

SEASONS
OF A
LEADER'S
LIFE

JEFF IORG

Learning, Leading, and
Leaving Your Legacy

SEASONS
OF A
LEADER'S
LIFE

NASHVILLE, TENNESSEE

978-1-4336-8150-9

Published by B&H Publishing Group
Nashville, Tennessee

Dewey Decimal Classification: 303.3
Subject Heading: PETER, APOSTLE \ LEADERSHIP \
LEARNING AND SCHOLARSHIP

1 2 3 4 5 6 7 • 17 16 15 14 13

With appreciation to mentors who were patient with me as a learner, helped me become a leader, and inspired me by their leadership legacy.

T. C. Melton
Burtis Williams
Casey Deshon
Cecil Sims
Bill Crews

CONTENTS

Part Two—Priorities for Active Leaders

Part Three—Convictions of Maturing Leaders

Part One

LESSONS FOR EMERGING LEADERS

INTRODUCTION

 My mentors are dying, and my students are younger than my children. I'm at an awkward age—I'm too old to appreciate today's music and too young to get the senior discount. From my mid-life vantage point, I see leaders living through various leadership seasons: all the way from teenagers just awakening to their destiny to statesmen wisely concluding years of effective service. I'm somewhere in the middle, a leader actively engaged in the prime challenge of making things happen, working with people all along the leadership continuum. I'm young enough to remember my formative years and old enough to be thinking about my legacy. Living through and observing others move through these seasons has motivated me to write this book. Hopefully it will help you make sense of the process, discover where you are in the leadership life cycle, and maximize the potential of your current leadership stage.

Life has seasons. For leaders, those seasons could also be called phases or stages of leadership. Younger leaders start out full of passion, idealistic, and excited about the future. Most of them are aware of how little they know about leadership and are zealous to learn all they can. They work hard to earn degrees, seek out mentors, attend conferences, read books, and so on. These emerging leaders recognize that their early years are primarily learning years—a time to gain information, solidify convictions, test theories, and practice skills. They discover the possibilities of their abilities and gain key insights about their future usefulness. This can be both an exciting and a trying time. While learning is the primary goal, many are also already leading (some with very significant responsibilities).

While good leaders are always learning, at some point the primacy of the learning phase gives way to the reality of the leading phase. Leading replaces learning as the main goal. This new season of life finds leaders engaged in their role, using their training to make a difference while still learning on the job. Leaders lead. They employ key practices to advance the mission of their organization. For Christian leaders, that means advancing the mission of God's kingdom as expressed uniquely through the commission of their church or ministry. Leaders who paid attention during the learning phase now have resources to draw from to know what to do. This longer season—sometimes decades long—is the prime of a leader's life when their most significant contributions are made.

But time marches on. Eventually, leaders recognize their time to lead is passing. Some make the mistake of holding on too long, dismantling what they have built by clinging to their leadership role long after their effectiveness has waned. Most leaders, however, are fully aware that the person in the mirror keeps getting older. For most of us, the loss of stamina alone forces us to face the reality that the final stage—the time to leave our legacy—is dawning. The final phase of a leader's life, the final contribution, is formalizing a leadership legacy. Some think of this in terms of a building, statue, or other tangible reminder of their contribution. Those can be meaningful. But a legacy is more than a thing or a place. Your legacy is the wisdom you have gained, the people you have influenced, and the convictions you modeled which inspire subsequent generations. Leaving a living legacy is more important than leaving a monument.

While the Bible contains many stories about great men, one leader in particular gives us a unique model of all three seasons. Peter lived through all three phases—learner, leader, and legacy-leaver—and stories from all three stages of his life are recorded in Scripture. In the Gospels, he was a learner; in the book of Acts, he was a leader; and in 1 and 2 Peter, he wrote his legacy.

This book looks at the stories of Peter's life through the lenses of these key questions:

- What was Peter learning about leadership?
- What do Peter's actions reveal about leadership?
- What did Peter write as his leadership legacy?

This book surveys the overarching story of Peter's ministry in Scripture, and examines leadership principles underlying the biblical narrative of Peter's life. We will be flying high, looking at the broadest perspective, and considering the big picture of what Peter's life teaches about learning, leading, and leaving a legacy.

This book is not a full commentary on Peter's life or the biblical texts describing it. While it takes the Bible seriously, its purpose isn't to exegete texts or critically analyze stories about Peter. Instead, it focuses on the previous three questions—considering one for each season of Peter's life—and isolates and applies the leadership principles that naturally emerge. This book doesn't cover every story involving Peter. Instead it focuses on the stories in which Peter is singled out by name, thus indicating his centrality to the narrative.

The first section of the book highlights every story in which Jesus singled out and interacted directly with Peter.

The second section examines every story in which Peter is portrayed or referenced as a leader, either in Acts or in the Epistles. Peter may have been present and providing leadership at other key points when the apostles are mentioned as a group, but for our purposes, the focus is on the stories in which Peter is a named character. The priority of his being named indicates the centrality of his participation and, thus, the potential to learn specifically from his leadership example.

The final section is different. It isn't based on stories about Peter. Instead, it summarizes what Peter wrote as his lasting legacy-gift to the church. The emphasis is on his legacy, not his activities or actions. His legacy is the wisdom he gained, the people he influenced, and the convictions he modeled for subsequent generations. Peter's legacy is so important, it became part of inspired Scripture. Your legacy won't achieve those lofty heights, but it's still an important capstone for your life.

While the book is divided into three neat sections, life isn't so regimented. The principles and insights in this book overlap from section to section. While there is a progression to a leader's experience, don't feel you must master every learning principle before you move on to leading. Some legacy decisions are made very early in life, even during the learning phase. This book is organized to help you think through leadership issues; it is not intended to be a step-by-step formula for your life. The book is also organized to stimulate further consideration of each topic. The chapters are short and to the point, more like essays on a theme than part of a longer treatise. Scripture passages are listed for each topic, and discussion questions are included. Take time to read the biblical material before reading each chapter. They are foundational to the leadership insights in the book. Some of the stories may be familiar, but setting the scriptural context is essential. As you read the passages, ask yourself the three questions previously mentioned. Each chapter summarizes at least one key insight from each text. Perhaps you will discover other principles that are instructive for your leadership journey.

Hopefully, this book will be an ideal resource for mentoring groups, reading groups, self-directed leadership development groups, staff improvement exercises, classroom readings, and organizational development for emerging leaders.

Learning, leading, and leaving your legacy. These are the phases of a leader's life. Which season are you in right now? What should you be learning? How can you improve what you are doing? What will you leave for future generations? Let's get started.

Lesson 1

ACCEPT YOUR IDENTITY

Matthew 10:1–4; Mark 6:7–13;
Luke 6:12–16; John 1:40–42

Becoming comfortable with being called a leader is an intimidating adjustment for many younger Christians. Even some seminary students tell me, "I don't really think of myself as a leader." They aren't yet comfortable with the mantle God has placed upon them. God-called, ministry-committed graduate students sometimes have a hard time accepting that they are supposed to be leaders.

These students readily identify themselves as being ministers, servants, missionaries, counselors, pastors, or active in various other ministry roles. But what they have a harder time accepting is that they are leaders. Part of God's call to leadership is to accept your new identity—a new definition of who you are and how you will live. Learning to lead begins with accepting your identity as a leader, even though you may not yet know all it will entail from the beginning.

Modern readers often view the lives of biblical characters backwards—from the end of the story instead of the beginning. We assume too much about their understanding of God's initial work in their lives because we have the benefit of spiritual hindsight. Because we know "the rest of the story" when we approach the biblical text, it's easy to assume that Peter knew from the start that he would be a great spiritual leader because of the remarkable leader he proved to be. That assumption isn't necessarily accurate. Until Peter met Jesus, he'd been more concerned with catching fish than kingdom leadership.

Andrew and Simon were brothers who operated an extensive commercial fishing operation with multiple boats and partners. Andrew wanted his brother to meet Jesus. He wanted Simon to experience the life-change that such a meeting could produce. He may have also wanted his brother, a business owner, to use his talents for different purposes. "We have found the Messiah," Andrew told Simon. Soon after that declaration, Andrew introduced Simon to Jesus.

Jesus met Simon (imagine the life-panorama Jesus might have visualized—knowing who Peter would become) and named him Cephas (Aramaic), which is translated Peter (Greek). Cephas, or Peter, means "the Rock." Jesus is identified as the Messiah, Simon as the Rock. Those are powerful titles describing unique roles for both men. While Jesus fully understood them, Peter didn't yet grasp all that Jesus meant by either title. Both titles reveal identity. Peter would come to fully understand Jesus' role as Messiah during the next three years. He would also begin a lifelong journey of understanding what it meant to be the rock of the early church.

Jesus inaugurated his relationship with Peter by giving him a new identity. Jesus changed Simon's name—a dramatic beginning to their relationship and a clear indication that Jesus intended to relate to Peter on new terms. Names have the power to shape character. I have a Native American friend who has both an Anglo name (to function in American culture) and a tribal name (related to the expectations his people have for him). Calling him by his tribal name evokes his heritage and motivates him to be a man of character and initiative. Calling him by that name is a call to action.

Names also have the power to reveal character. This is one of the reasons God is known by so many names in the Bible. God's nature is too complex to be described with only one name, so he has dozens of names, both descriptive and proactive. When Jesus changed Simon's name to Peter, he created a goal for Peter to mature toward and an expectation of progress for his disciple.

While the full impact of his new name wouldn't become evident to Peter for many years, it must have struck him as powerfully significant that Jesus would change his name at their first meeting. What did this mean? Why such a dramatic declaration? He hadn't assumed his leadership identity or any specific leadership role; that would come much later. Nevertheless, when Peter met Jesus, his identity as a leader was both revealed and shaped by the new name he was given.

Beyond this initial encounter in which Peter was called as a leader, it's also evident Jesus intended him to be *the* leader of the original twelve disciples. Whenever the Twelve are mentioned in the Bible, Peter is always listed first. Similarly, when small groups of three or four disciples are mentioned, Peter is usually mentioned first or portrayed as the leader. Peter was a leader of leaders.

Many younger leaders have a more difficult time accepting this assignment—leading leaders—than even answering the simple call to lead. Yet God expects some to be leaders of leaders. This is the only way any organization, including the church and other ministries, can grow. Whether it is a church-planting movement, an inner-city recovery ministry, or a suburban mega church—all large organizations require layers of leaders to enlarge their impact. God calls some to lead, some to lead leaders, and some to lead many leaders.

Why is a leadership identity so hard to accept? There are four common reasons young leaders struggle to accept their new identity.

First, some struggle to accept their identity as leaders because of false humility. They believe that "I am a leader" is a prideful statement. It isn't. Agreeing with God that you are a leader is simply accepting and affirming his assignment for you. In a sense, denying your role as a leader is prideful, since you make yourself the final authority and reject God's plan for you. Accepting your assignment demonstrates humility, not pride.

Related to this are the struggles that some younger believers have with formal expressions of authority or organizational structure. Both are sometimes (wrongly) considered impediments to true spiritual community. I have noticed recently that some younger ministry leaders seem determined to do everything by collaboration, conversation, and coffee. That's an overreaction—a leadership cop-out—that limits kingdom growth. Have you noticed leading technology companies, who employ so many post-moderns, have no trouble creating structure and expressing authority through making decisions that result in worldwide impact? So why do we? Why is this post-modern aversion to leading through structure mostly evident among younger *ministry* leaders? Don't buy into the myth that true community lacks structure or is inhibited by formally recognizing some people as the leaders.

Younger leaders may also struggle to accept their new identity because they feel inadequate to lead. Inadequacy isn't a disqualifying characteristic. If it were, God wouldn't have any leaders. Younger leaders often idealize the character and skills required to lead. They measure themselves by the more mature leadership qualities of their mentors. What younger leaders fail to realize is that their mentors were much like them when they were the same age. They had limited skills and were still working through character formation issues. God calls and uses imperfect people in leadership. Don't be intimidated by comparing yourself to those far more experienced than you are.

Lastly, younger leaders may resist accepting their new identity because they fear the responsibility it brings. While learning to lead, new leaders observe their mentors and the responsibility they bear. The load can seem overwhelming. God is gracious, however, in doling out leadership responsibility. He has a wonderful way of matching leadership responsibility with leadership development. As you grow in your capacity to lead, God will increase your leadership responsibility proportionately. Don't fear the burden of leadership. God will give you responsibility in proportion to your readiness to shoulder the burden of leadership.

God also works through the burden of leading to increase your capacity for leadership. For example, as a young pastor, I had to pray and trust God for several hundred thousand dollars for a church building program. Later, in another ministry, I grew to trust God for a few million dollars. Now I am responsible for a multimillion-dollar budget and am attempting to develop new projects that require millions more. God equipped me for this present challenge by growing me through those earlier leadership experiences.

Simon became Peter, the kingdom leader. The fisherman became the rock. Meeting Jesus and accepting his new identity changed everything for Peter. It's the same for you. You have sensed Jesus directing you to lead his people, to take new responsibility. Accept your new identity. Get comfortable wearing the leadership mantle. Commit to the journey of discovering the full meaning of your new identity.

QUESTIONS FOR REFLECTION

1. Have you fully accepted your identity as a leader, or are you still in the process of doing so?
2. What barriers do you need to overcome to accept your identity as a leader?
3. How is your leadership identity developing or changing at this point in your life?

PROCESS YOUR CALL

Matthew 4:18–20; Mark 1:16–18

 Learning to lead begins with understanding your call to ministry leadership. The difficulty of gaining that understanding is compounded by the different ways Christians talk about being called. The many ways the words *call* or *calling* are used in popular culture also confuses the issue. Emerging leaders often struggle to reconcile their own unsettled experience with the confident ease so many veteran leaders seem to have about their call.

The concept of a call means different things in different contexts. For example, an important phone call may bring news of the birth of a child or a job offer. A person may be called up to active duty in the military or to the varsity from a lower team. Professionals like physicians, teachers, and counselors might pursue their occupation as a calling, with an inner drive that eclipses external rewards.

These varied uses of the word *call* have two things in common. They communicate new information and bestow new responsibility. Being called into ministry leadership is similar. You have new information, and God directs you to a new role. You have new responsibility; God assigns you new work.

As described in chapter one, Andrew introduced Peter to Jesus. That meeting established Peter's new identity and initiated the call process. Prior to and for some time after their first meeting with Jesus, Peter and Andrew continued working as commercial fishermen. There came a time, however, when closing down the fishing business and moving toward ministry leadership became the priority. It may have been as much as a year after their first meeting that Jesus called Peter in this way. Perhaps Jesus and Peter had several encounters over the few months after they first met, finally culminating in Peter's definitive call to focus entirely on ministry leadership.

There is some question about how many times Jesus met Peter and called him, using the context of fishing. Two gospel writers, Matthew and Mark, tell about one of these incidents. Some commentators see Luke's version as an expansion of the same story. Others see it as a distinctive, second incident. Either way, we can see that—whether Luke expands on a single incident or there were two incidents—the same point can be made here. Jesus' call of Peter was a process that probably involved a series of encounters. Emerging leaders often struggle to resolve issues related to their call. They sense they are called, but to what? They feel called to lead, but how? When are they supposed to start? What are they supposed to do? Answers are elusive. Younger leaders wonder if processing their call—understanding it in fits and starts—is abnormal and somehow dishonoring to God.

Most emerging leaders don't have a precise understanding of their call based on one dramatic revelation from God. Based on Peter's example and experience, emerging leaders often go through a process to fully understand God's call. You are normal if you are experiencing your call in phases, or stages, or layers of progressive understanding.

When God calls, you answer—as much as you know how. Then you learn more about God and yourself. God clarifies his call; you understand it more fully; and you respond more definitively. Eventually, you understand God's call clearly enough to leave behind all other options and serve him in your assigned leadership role.

Take solace in Peter's experience. Peter made progress in understanding and following Jesus. He went through a process, over time, before he responded fully. If you are having the same experience, cooperate with the process and be patient. You're normal!

Another vexing problem for emerging leaders is defining God's call. How, from a biblical perspective, is calling defined? In my previous book, *Is God Calling Me?*, I defined it this way: A call is a profound impression from God that establishes parameters for your life and can only be changed by a subsequent superseding impression from God. Some insights about God's call emerge from this definition.

First, a call is *a profound impression from God*. It's an inner urging or a persistent prompting that won't go away. A calling is a settled conviction that God wants you to do something. It is a feeling, yes. But it's more than an emotional moment. It's a soul-burning passion that you cannot escape and can only satisfy through obedience. No matter the means of your calling, the conclusion is experiential—you know it in your heart. That conclusion defies critical analysis. Being called is more intuitive than analytic. No matter how much data you collect, you must ultimately reconcile that information with what you know in your heart. Discerning a call to ministry leadership is a profoundly spiritual process. What happens is deep, mysterious, and long-lasting. Sometimes it comes through great pain or personal struggle. Like Jacob wrestling with the Angel of the Lord, your inner battle to obey God can feel like hand-to-hand combat. Other times, it can seem like a sweet release as you are liberated to follow God's best plan. In either case, being called is a profound impression from God.

Second, a call *establishes parameters for your life*. Like giant guardrails, a calling protects you and guides your behavior. A calling means you say yes to some things and no to others. When God calls, other life choices must be made in the context of answering the call. Anything incompatible with obedience must be rejected in pursuit of the call.

For example, God called me to ministry leadership before I met my wife, Ann. When we started dating, we had to settle an important issue early in our relationship. I couldn't date anyone who didn't have a similar call to ministry. As it turned out, Ann had the same conviction. We soon discovered we shared a similar calling, and that granted us both the freedom to pursue our relationship.

Several seminary students have shared painful stories of having to end relationships with potential life partners who didn't share their call. One woman told me, "God has called me to give my life in China. Leaving my college boyfriend over that issue was the single hardest decision I have ever made." A young man sobbed deeply as he told of being dumped by his high school sweetheart after God called him, while in college, to be a pastor.

These parameters aren't just relational. A missionary interviewed for a faculty position at a seminary but then withdrew from the process, saying, "God called me to be a missionary, not to teach missions. I just can't leave the field." Another person turned down lucrative secular employment, saying, "My call is to full-time ministry leadership. No distractions or temptations allowed." These people recognized the different but very real parameters put in place by their call from God.

A clear sense of call means more than always saying no. It also informs our "yeses." A college student reported, "God has called me to teach—my passion is junior high kids." She is in college preparing to pursue God's call. A veteran pastor recently resigned a twenty-year pastorate to return to seminary. Why? God has called him to teach, and he needed additional academic preparation. Your calling establishes parameters, giant brackets around your life, which informs your choices and directs the outcome of your life.

Third, a call *can only be changed by a subsequent, superseding impression from God.* When God calls, you pursue the call until he calls you to something else. When God calls, you stay put until God moves you. This has two implications. First, God-called people pursue their ministry as a calling, not a career. We aren't looking for a bigger position, a higher paycheck, or a more prestigious situation. We are called, and we serve to fulfill our calling. Second, being called means you persevere through tough times. God-called men and women don't quit when circumstances are difficult. God-called people stay put; firmly planted until they receive a subsequent, superseding call to a new assignment.

God not only calls us to ministry leadership but also to specific assignments of ministry responsibility. One person told me, "God calls generally to ministry leadership, but a pastorate is just a job. Get the best one you can." To me, that cheapens our understanding of the high office of pastoral leadership. God not only calls generally to ministry leadership, but he calls specifically to ministry assignments. A general call to ministry leadership is a lifelong commitment. Your specific assignment may change several times over a lifetime.

God called Peter to lead. Eventually Peter answered the call and fully devoted himself to Jesus. Some criticize Peter unduly, citing his spiritual dullness and slowness to leave fishing and serve a higher purpose. Peter wasn't dull or distracted. He was a normal man processing significant new spiritual information and moving steadily toward a life fully devoted to kingdom leadership. Like Peter, you will most likely move through a process of understanding God's call. Don't despair if you are in the middle of this process. Keep listening! Sense the direction and guidance of the Holy Spirit. Ask God to continue to clarify his call in your life—and obey him fully each step of the way.

QUESTIONS FOR REFLECTION

1. Where are you in the process of understanding your call to ministry leadership?
2. What are some parameters placed on your life because of God's call?
3. Do you agree that God calls us to specific ministry assignments? Why or why not?

Lesson 3

SETTLE YOUR CALL

Luke 5:1–11

Understanding God's call is a process; settling your call requires a decision. At a moment in time, you must say, "Yes, Lord." Peter's calling process culminated during a specific encounter with Jesus when he made the choice to settle his call once and for all.

Peter and his partners had fished all night, and they had nothing to show for it but tired backs and bloodshot eyes. They were mending their nets, getting ready to store their boats, and catch some sleep. Jesus climbed into one of the boats and started teaching the crowd. After a while, he told Peter, "Put out into deep water and let down your nets for a catch."

Seemingly resigned to limited possibilities, Peter replied, "Master . . . at Your word, I'll let down the nets." The nets were reloaded and the boats launched. Perhaps with some grumbling, the men rowed out to deep water. A huge catch resulted! Partners and another boat were summoned. The fish filled both boats so full that they began to sink. What a joyous moment for everyone!

Well, almost everyone. Peter's response reveals how deeply the experience moved him. "Go away from me, because I'm a sinful man, Lord," Peter lamented. He was undone; he described himself as sinful—scum, filth, trash. One use of the root word for sinful is "shoe scraping." Peter had debased himself in powerful terms.

Jesus used the occasion to affirm rather than condemn Peter. In spite of Peter's inadequacy, Jesus told him, "Don't be afraid." That's an idiom that could be translated, "Don't let that limit or control you." Then Jesus told Peter, "From now on you will be catching people!"

No further verbal response from Peter or the disciples is recorded. Instead, their actions speak louder than words: "Then they brought the boats to land, left everything, and followed Him." This was Peter's moment of total commitment to kingdom leadership. Jesus spoke to Peter about fishing and following him. The juxtaposition of the miracle and the moment sealed Peter's obedience. He saw Jesus for who he was; he saw himself for who he really was; and the kingdom mission became his new priority. He "left everything" and followed Jesus. Peter had the privilege of a face-to-face relationship with Jesus. He knew the sound of Jesus' voice and the power of his words. Hence, when Jesus said, "Let down your nets," Peter was willing to take action on a word from Jesus.

This is the essence of responding to God's call to ministry leadership. You hear from God through various means, and you answer affirmatively. Peter knew Jesus personally and heard him speak audibly. God still speaks today, but not the same way he did through Jesus to Peter. So how does God communicate his callings to us today?

Surveying the range of call experiences in the Bible, we see three general ways that God calls people. It's important to understand the different ways God calls and to affirm the legitimacy of his various methods. "Calling" often evokes images of Moses' burning bush or Paul's blinding light as the primary or preferred method. You may wonder if that's the kind of experience you should expect. Possibly, but probably not.

The following are not rigid categories; you may experience one or more of these or a combination of them over a lifetime. There is no right or preferred way to be called. God called in various ways in the Bible, and he still does so today.

First, God calls through sudden experiences. God appeared to Moses in a desert and to Paul on a road. Both were sudden, dramatic, and spiritually overwhelming experiences. God sometimes calls like this today. One leader said to me, "God simply filled the room where I was praying. I had an overwhelming sense of his presence. He spoke to me as clearly as a person might speak in a conversation." God still calls through profound, powerful, supernatural encounters.

Sometimes these experiences take place in private. Other times, they occur during corporate worship. God may speak clearly during a personal crisis, using the brokenness resulting from the experience to create spiritual openness. By various means, God speaks, and somehow we know it's *his* voice. The distinctive characteristic of a call through a sudden experience is the overwhelming sense of God's presence. While you may have difficulty explaining it, you are absolutely sure of what happened to you.

Second, God calls through reasoned decisions. Sometimes, God allows us to work through a process to discover his call. The validity of this means is often difficult to accept. We want a dramatic experience and might feel less than spiritual if our call results from a reasoned or reasonable decision.

A reasoned process, however, is a frequent means of discovering God's call. One striking example: Paul and his team were traveling "through the region of Phrygia and Galatia and were prevented by the Holy Spirit from speaking . . . in Asia. When they came to Mysia, they tried to go into Bithynia, but the Spirit of Jesus did not allow them. So, bypassing Mysia, they came down to Troas" (Acts 16:6–8). That was a lot of walking around trying to find the next opening for the gospel. It probably took weeks, maybe months, to sort out the direction they were supposed to go.

This was definitely a reasoned process. The answer to their question, "God, where are you calling us to go next with the gospel?" was not written in the sky or revealed by an angel. It was discovered slowly, through trial and error, as the missionary team walked from city to city, looking for an opening for their message.

Finally, after arriving in Troas, Paul had a dream in which a man from Macedonia asked for help. If God wanted them in Macedonia, why hadn't he put this dream in Paul's mind weeks before? God must have intended for the team to walk a while as part of the discovery process. Perhaps the walking and waiting process was part of Paul's becoming open to receiving the final word through the dream.

Paul and his team worked through a lengthy process to find where to plant the gospel in Europe. God sometimes calls through reasoned decisions made by search committees, trustee boards, and others who work through tedious decision-making processes. God also calls through reasoned decisions as leaders analyze population trends, cultural indicators, and spiritual needs.

My call to church planting was a reasoned decision. For months, we investigated the possibilities before finally settling on an area near Portland, Oregon. God never gave us a dramatic experience to confirm this call—there was no burning bush or blinding light. But over time, through careful consideration of our gifts, a burden about the need, and alignment of our life circumstances, we knew God was calling us.

Third, God calls through the prompting of others. David experienced this when he was called to be king. Samuel showed up, summoned David, and announced that he was God's chosen one (1 Sam. 16:1–13). In Acts 13:2, the Holy Spirit told the church to set apart Paul and Barnabas for missionary work. The missionary team was sitting in the service—why didn't the Spirit just tell them? The text is quite specific. The message came through the church to the missionaries.

God may prompt a friend, a church member, a candidate consultant from a mission board, or a fellow leader to speak his call to you. God sometimes calls by sending a messenger to encourage us to consider a specific ministry assignment. The first indication that God was calling me to Golden Gate Seminary came when a close friend told me, "I believe God is going to call you to be president of Golden Gate, and you need to prepare yourself for that responsibility."

Most churches and Christian institutions use a committee, board, or collaborative process to choose leaders. This is sometimes criticized as cumbersome and bureaucratic. In reality, it recognizes that God often speaks through others to reveal his call. Although my friend was the first to speak to me about becoming a seminary president, it was comforting to know it wouldn't happen unless the trustees agreed that God was calling me. This isn't sub-spiritual bureaucracy thwarting or slowing God's work. It's reassuring dependence on the collective wisdom of the church expressed through people with the authority and responsibility to make the right decision. We should celebrate the checks and balances that a process like this affords rather than rail against it as contravening God's call.

God calls through sudden experiences, reasoned decisions, and the prompting of others. While fully understanding God's call may be a process, responding to his call requires a specific decision. Eventually, Peter "left everything and followed Him."

The phrase "left everything" is all-encompassing. Certainly, Peter left his fishing business behind. But he left much more than boats and nets. Peter left his livelihood and his hope for providing for his family. He left his retirement plan—building a business and passing it to his family who would care for him in his later years. He left his source of community and esteem as a fisherman who provided for the villages in the area. Peter left his friendships—the camaraderie of fishing competitors, dockworkers, netmakers, fishmongers, and customers. Peter left everything!

Obeying God's call may require you to leave behind people, places, and things that are dear to you but incompatible with the call. Missionaries, for example, leave their extended families to serve in distant locations. Holiday celebrations are missed, aging parents must be cared for by others, cousins grow up not knowing each other, and grandchildren miss the blessing of generational mentoring. Following God may mean you won't be near the comforts of home. Certain foods, regional dialects, hospitality habits, and other cultural mores that make you feel at home may be sacrificed to answer your calling. These sacrifices are part of your obedience to God in fulfilling your calling.

God's call to ministry leadership may also mean that you will give up material things you might have otherwise had. Ministry leaders usually sacrifice financially to work in churches, missions, or ministry organizations. Our compensation is often less than that of others with similar education and responsibility. We choose to live on less, give away more, and model a frugal lifestyle as part of answering God's call.

Most of us haven't left everything like Peter did, but we have left behind significant relationships, comfortable locations, and precious possessions to pursue God's call. Don't feel sorry for yourself because you have made those choices. Pursuing God's call requires sacrifice—it always has; it always will.

Experiencing God's call may be a process, but answering his call requires a definite decision. If you know God is calling you to ministry leadership or to a specific ministry assignment, say yes. Delayed obedience is disobedience. Say yes now.

QUESTIONS FOR REFLECTION

1. Was your call to ministry leadership a sudden experience, a reasoned decision, or did it come through the prompting of others? Was it a combination of these?
2. What have you sacrificed to pursue God's call? What is your attitude about this?
3. Are you fully obeying God's call in your life? If not, why not?

Lesson 4

GOD PROVIDES

Matthew 8:14–15; Mark 1:29–31; Luke 4:38–39;
Matthew 17:24–27; Luke 22:7–13

 Early in Peter's relationship with Jesus, he learned an essential lesson for ministry leaders: God provides. Jesus taught Peter this lesson through two separate incidents at Capernaum, along with a later reminder just before his last meal with the disciples.

Jesus launched his teaching ministry in the Capernaum synagogue. After a service, he went to Peter's house and healed his mother-in-law. Through this experience, Jesus taught Peter an important lesson about ministry leadership. As a family man in a patriarchal culture, Peter had familial responsibilities. Jesus showed Peter he would meet the practical needs of his family.

Peter had recently given up his fishing business and was now Jesus' itinerant disciple. As Peter considered leaving his business, he probably wondered how he would meet the needs of his family without his business income. Jesus used this healing opportunity as a teaching moment to settle the issue for Peter. The lesson was clear: God provides for ministry leaders by meeting their personal needs.

The second incident that confirmed God's provision happened sometime later, also at Capernaum. Peter was asked to pay a two-drachma temple tax, but he questioned the legitimacy of doing so. Jesus told him to pay the tax but promised to provide the money in an unusual way. He told Peter to go to the sea and cast a fishhook (not a net) to catch just one fish. In its mouth would be a coin providing the amount needed to pay the tax for both Jesus and Peter. What a remarkable means of provision! Catch a fish, open its mouth, take out coin, and pay the tax—a set of unusual circumstances clearly designed more to teach a principle than just to provide the money. Ministry leaders have practical responsibilities, including financial obligations that must be met. The time demands of leadership coupled with often minimal compensation for ministry leaders makes meeting practical responsibilities challenging. Jesus promises to meet our financial needs when we follow him.

Early in my pastoral ministry, we had limited income and maximum family demands. Our church was a relatively small, working-class congregation, so my salary was modest. We lived from paycheck to paycheck, supporting a preschooler and a baby. One morning, our refrigerator quit.

An older gentleman had visited our church a few times at the invitation of his banker, Ken, who was also a member of our church. Soon after I met him, he was diagnosed with cancer and hospitalized in terminal condition. Ken took time off from work to care for this friend. I visited him in the hospital regularly. He passed away the same morning our refrigerator conked out.

I told Ann, "Buy some ice and pack the baby formula and other essentials in a cooler. Tomorrow or the next day, after the funeral, I will try to find a used refrigerator." She agreed, making the best of a tough situation. I spent that day handling funeral arrangements and getting ready for the upcoming service.

The following morning, Ken called. "Can you come by the bank first thing this morning? I need to see you." As busy as I was, I assumed he was grieving and probably wanted a pastoral visit prior to the service. Ken welcomed me into his office and said, "My friend really appreciated your kindness toward him, even though he wasn't a member of our church. A few days ago, he wrote this check for you and asked me to give it to you immediately after his death."

The check was for $500. I called Ann and said, "Change of plans on the refrigerator." We bought a brand new one—for $495—and marveled once again at God's amazing, miraculous provision.

Over the years, we have tried to catalog God's provision—to make sense of where the money or other support has come from so we could celebrate it. Sometimes it was clear. But more times than not, we have looked at each other and asked, "How did we manage that?" Through a combination of provision and protection, God has kept our family fed, clothed, and sheltered—plus he's provided additional resources for extras like vacations and college educations.

"God provides" is an important lesson for younger leaders and a continuing lesson for all leaders. Seminary students usually live on limited means yet seldom complain. They know that young adulthood is a season of emerging responsibilities. Learning to trust God for themselves—not trusting others who trust God on their behalf—is part of growing up. When a student reports, "My car broke down, and the same day I got a check in the mail from a family in my home church that just covered it," I smile. That's God teaching an important leadership lesson that no school curriculum can include.

While learning to trust God's provision starts early in ministry leadership, it's also a never-ending process. Near the end of their time together, Jesus reminded Peter of his provision by instructing him on preparing for their final meal. Peter was told to find a man with a water jug, follow him to a house, and tell the owner that Jesus needed a place to eat with his disciples. Peter did so and *voila!* Room and provisions for a banquet were miraculously provided. No matter the need, Jesus provides everything necessary to accomplish his purposes.

The broader the leadership responsibility, the more it takes to fund the enterprise. The larger the scope of the ministry, the more money is needed. In the early days, all I needed was one refrigerator. Now my responsibilities demand much more.

At one time, I thought I would eventually grow to the point where I would no longer fret about money. I would have discovered the key to always having all the money needed to fund whatever ministry I was leading. Along the way, however, it dawned on me how unlikely this would ever be. God doesn't want me to have all the money needed—personally or professionally. He wants me to trust him, in the moment, to provide. By doing so, he accomplishes several objectives. He hones my spiritual edge. He controls the timing and pace of ministry advance. He makes it clear it's his ministry. And, most important, he gets all the glory.

God provides for what he wants done—not what we want to do for him. When no provision is evident, a wise leader considers carefully if God really wants the project in question done. God provides—but he also withholds provision to keep things from happening. After I explained this at some length in a chapel sermon, a student responded, "I can summarize your message in five words: God's will equals God's bill." It had taken me forty minutes to communicate the message contained in those five words!

Emerging leaders must learn this foundational lesson: God provides. He will structure your resources to make sure you trust him. He will limit your income, increase your family demands, broaden your professional responsibilities, and enlarge your vision to create financial tension. As you emerge a leader, God is teaching you. Learn the lessons well and remember the stories of his provision. Like our refrigerator story, you will have your own examples reminding you of God's past provision—which is the best indicator of his future ability to provide.

God called a younger leader, Meredith, to an independently funded missionary position. She prayed and told her friends about the need. They told other friends, and then she started asking for offerings. "What happens," she asked, "if the money doesn't come in?" "Simple," I replied, "God doesn't want you to go. But let's assume that the opportunity you have discovered is from God and see what happens." Within months, she was fully funded and on the mission field. More important than the money, however, was the lesson she learned: God provides.

Do you wonder where the money will come from for your ministry? Do you wonder how you will support your family? If you become a ministry leader, do you fear your family will face financial hardship? These are legitimate concerns. God teaches younger leaders to trust him by providing for them, often in unusual ways like fishy coins and free refrigerators. Learning to trust God for his provision—for both your family and your ministry—is a foundational lesson for long-term leadership effectiveness.

QUESTIONS FOR REFLECTION

1. How has God provided for you in the past? Keep a record of these stories to share with your followers.
2. What are you trusting God to provide right now? How is this training you for your future leadership role?
3. When God withholds provision, what does this mean to you? Why?

Lesson 5

DEVELOP SPIRITUAL DISCIPLINES

Mark 1:35–39; Mark 3:13–19; Luke 6:12–16;
Matthew 17:1–13; Mark 9:2–13; Luke 9:28–36

 A dirty little secret about Christian leadership is how many leaders are running on empty, foregoing spiritual disciplines and depending on fleshly activity to fake ministerial effectiveness. It's a fool's errand—yet an all-too-common reality. Many leaders ignore prayer and Bible reading, neglect fasting and worship, and are too busy to honor the biblical pattern of Sabbath rest. Jesus emphasized in several interactions with Peter the importance of these and other spiritual practices. Jesus prayed, fasted, worshipped, spent time alone with God, and went away for personal retreats. Peter had been a commercial fisherman, a man's man who worked hard and depended on physical strength. Jesus modeled tapping a different power source.

Jesus slipped away one morning for private prayer. Peter led a search party to find him and let him know the crowds were looking for him. Jesus didn't rebuke Peter for interrupting him. He agreed it was time to return to public ministry. Peter seemed a bit impatient in his search, wanting Jesus to get busy helping people. But Jesus modeled an important pattern for Peter: private prayer precedes public preaching.

A short time later, Jesus went away to pray through the night. Afterwards, he summoned the Twelve and appointed them to a special ministry assignment—he sent them on a preaching, healing, and exorcizing tour. Peter observed this pattern: pray first, then select and send out workers.

On another occasion, Jesus went to a mountain to pray. He took Peter, along with James and John. While the other fellows took a nap, Jesus prayed. His appearance was transformed and two heavenly men, Moses and Elijah, communed with him. Peter woke up the other two disciples, observed the splendor of the meeting, and offered to put up three temporary tabernacles. He intended to stay on the mountain for a while. He finally seemed to understand the importance of spiritual discipline and devotion, of retreating to connect with God's presence. He wanted to stay on the mountain.

But God had other plans. He affirmed Jesus to the apostolic trio, saying, "This is My Son, the Chosen One, listen to Him!" Then God sent them down the mountain, plunging them into ministry among a large crowd gathered around a father desperately looking for deliverance for his demon-possessed son. The power of God experienced on the mountain was demonstrated in the valley. Peter observed this principle: spending time with God produces power for public ministry.

Many emerging leaders are overwhelmed with the demands of school or other training programs, navigating young adulthood, and simply making life work. There are jobs, romantic relationships or new spouses, and growing ministries; along with school, financial, and family demands. These pressures make it difficult to maintain disciplines like daily devotions, weekly worship and rest, or periodic retreats for spiritual recovery. Younger leaders tell themselves that life is too demanding. They promise themselves that they'll get back to the disciplines after school is out or after the wedding is over or the first child is born or the children start school or the job settles down or once the ministry becomes more manageable. But the devil is lying to them.

Life doesn't get easier or less demanding or less complicated as you get older. Don't assume, just because you're facing many challenges for the first time, that life won't always be so demanding. It can be, and it is. As you move through the learning phase, a subtext to these other lessons is

"do it now." If something is important, get started doing it now—not later.
It isn't going to get any easier.

Part of the challenge of establishing spiritual disciplines when life is
demanding is just that—they are most essential when life is demanding.
Jesus had more important work to do than anyone in human history. He
had few helpers and was confronted by overwhelming needs. Yet he prioritized private time alone with his Father. Like Peter, we must learn to do
the same thing. The patterns we establish during the learning phase will
sustain us when responsibilities intensify in the leadership phase.

What, then, are the essential spiritual disciplines you should establish
during the learning season of your life? Here are five nonnegotiables:

Bible reading. Many leaders read or study the Bible in order to teach it
to others. That's great, but don't fall into the trap of only reading the Bible
for others. Read it for yourself. Develop the discipline of systematically
reading through the Bible, asking God to speak to you. Ask for insight
about your life and ministry. Keep the focus on your needs. God will occasionally give you an insight leading to a sermon, Bible study, or help for
a counselee. But that's not the purpose of devotional Bible reading. Read
the Bible for personal insight, correction, instruction, and encouragement.

Prayer. Meeting with others to pray is a good practice. But again,
don't let it replace private prayer time. As a leader, you certainly need to
pray about your needs and your ministry's needs. Intercession for others is
essential. Praying about ministry dilemmas and decisions is important. But
don't forget to pray for yourself and your family. Use the insights from your
Bible reading to guide your prayer time. Ask God to change you in ways
he reveals as you read Scripture.

Fasting. Skipping meals for spiritual purposes is a powerful way to
focus your spiritual devotion. This has been an interesting aspect of my
spiritual development. This is the only spiritual discipline which was actually stronger in my life as a younger leader than it is now. (That's just to let
you know, I'm still learning!) Fasting from things other than food—like
sexual activity, technology, or entertainment—can also sharpen your spiritual devotion.

Worship. While private Bible study and prayer are essential, corporate
worship is also vital. Leaders need the occasional experience of participating in worship, not always leading worship. Leaders need to hear the Word

proclaimed, share group prayer, feel the power of congregational singing, and experience the accountability of being present for worship.

Rest. Working six days and resting one is the scriptural pattern. This is the most oft-neglected spiritual discipline for leaders. We are, quite often, workaholics determined to impress God and earn his favor by our efforts. Self-sacrifice is admirable. Working yourself into burnout isn't. Jesus modeled rest. He went away to pray, enjoyed personal retreats, and set aside the needs of the crowds to refresh himself spiritually.

Why is rest so difficult for leaders? Two reasons. First, we are convinced that ministerial effectiveness depends on our efforts. That's arrogance. Second, we don't believe God can accomplish as much in six days as we can do for him in seven. That's self-absorption. Those aren't good qualities for leaders. Making the decision to practice Sabbath rest is a spiritual choice. It requires faith to trust God to get his work done through us. It requires discipline to order six days for maximum productivity. Resting isn't a matter of finding more time, but of disciplined faith.

As you develop spiritual habits, learn to distinguish between consistency and perfection. As a younger leader, I wallowed in false guilt over my inability to practice these disciplines perfectly. Sometimes I just gave up and quit altogether. In my warped thinking, if perfection was unattainable, then what was the point of trying? As I matured in my understanding of God's grace, deepened my security in him, and fought through deadening legalism, my perspective changed.

Practicing the disciplines regularly, not perfectly, became my new goal. I confess—I don't always read the Bible or pray every day. I still miss some days. I practice Sabbath rest between forty and forty-five weeks a year. My schedule gets out of control sometimes. Fasting, as already mentioned, is still a challenge. Worship, since I'm almost always a worship leader, requires effort to find ways to do it.

My goal is consistency, not perfection,. I strive to practicing the disciplines daily or regularly as most appropriate. When I fail to reach those goals, I no longer beat myself up with false guilt. I confess my inadequacy, ask God for his strength, and pick up again the next day. While that was a simple sentence to write, it took about a decade to learn the lesson. I know you will do better.

QUESTIONS FOR REFLECTION

1. Which spiritual discipline is most difficult for you? What are you doing to strengthen this area?
2. How do you respond to this statement about the disciplines: "Strive for consistency, not perfection"? Is legalism about spiritual disciplines a problem for you?
3. Do you have realistic expectations about your practice of spiritual disciplines? If not, how will you adjust them?

Lesson 6

TRUST GOD'S POWER

Matthew 9:18–26; Mark 5:21–43; Luke 8:40–56

 Christian leaders often attempt what seems impossible. We plant churches, start schools, open new mission fields, build facilities, and raise large amounts of money for all types of projects. We also help alcoholics quit the bottle, pornographers recover their purity, adulterers rekindle their marriages, homosexuals reorient their lifestyles, and incest victims learn to trust again. Ministry challenges are daunting. Rather than accept the status quo, we must acknowledge our limitations and then access God's power to accomplish supernatural results.

When we take on these obstacles to kingdom growth or personal wholeness, we aren't always trusted by our followers. We certainly aren't encouraged by those outside the faith. We aren't always appreciated when we confront these challenges—nevertheless, we press on, accessing God's power to do what seems impossible. God demonstrates his power through emerging leaders, not just to meet their immediate needs but also to increase their confidence in him for the long haul. Peter learned these lessons firsthand, both among the crowd and then in private.

Jesus consigned some demons into a herd of pigs (rough day for the pigs!). Rather than celebrate the supernatural results, the onlookers encouraged Jesus to move on. That response set the stage for what was to follow—a further contrast between welcoming and ridiculing those who trust the power of God. As Jesus arrived at the next ministry site, a man named Jairus fought his way through the crowd. He appealed to Jesus, pleading from his knees for Jesus to come to his home and heal his sick daughter. Twelve years old was too young to die! He desperately wanted Jesus to intervene and deliver his precious little girl.

Jesus agreed to see her and began making his way through the dense crowd. A woman brushed against him. Jesus stopped and asked, "Who touched Me?" Before anyone stepped forward, Peter essentially said, "Lord, a lot of people are touching you. What difference does it make?" Jesus was undeterred. "Power has gone out from Me," he said, and he wanted to meet the recipient. A woman who had suffered a twelve-year hemorrhage stepped forward. Fearful yet grateful, she explained her situation and confessed having touched Jesus' robe. "Your faith has made you well," Jesus told her. "Go in peace."

While that story illustrates Jesus' power to heal, it is also a precursor to the more dramatic event about to happen. The delay caused by working through the crowd and healing the hemorrhagic woman resulted in the death of Jairus' daughter. Some messengers arrived with the news, indicating Jesus was no longer needed since the girl was dead. Jesus wasn't dissuaded. He continued his journey, telling those around him to "only believe."

When Jesus arrived at Jairus' house, mourning was already underway. A large crowd had gathered, spilling out of the house where the girl's body lay. When Jesus announced, "She is not dead but asleep," the crowd laughed at him. They laughed at Jesus! He could cast demons into pigs and help a bleeding woman with a touch of his robe, sure—but bring a girl back to life? That was beyond what anyone could do—even Jesus. To think otherwise was ludicrous. Who could overcome the power of death?

Jesus emptied the house of the crowd; allowing only Peter, James, John, and Jairus and his wife to stay with the girl's body. Jesus spoke a simple command/prayer, "Child, get up." She did. Peter had now experienced God's power at work through Jesus in three ways—casting demons out of pigs, healing a woman in a crowd, and now restoring a girl to life.

In the first instance, those who saw the pigs die feared God's power and asked Jesus to leave the area. In the second case, no one except Jesus recognized what had been accomplished by God's power. Finally, when Jesus promised to do the truly miraculous—bring a girl back to life—people laughed at him.

These are still common responses people have to God's power to intervene in human affairs. Some want to avoid it; some want to ignore it; and others laugh when a leader challenges them to trust God for the impossible. Emerging leaders must develop this unshakable conviction: have confidence in God's power. Trust God no matter how impossible, improbable, or unlikely it seems. Trust God to accomplish what people say can't be done. Trust Him to change people, to deliver them from all kinds of chaotic life situations.

J. W. was dying. He had a series of health problems and had been through all sorts of medical treatments. Nothing had worked. He was comatose. His family had assembled, and they called me to make one final hospital visit. His wife asked me to anoint J. W. with oil and pray for him to be healed, saying, "It's what the Bible says, and we should have done it long ago." I recognized her desperation. I explained there was no magic in the oil. I knew she was grieving, seemingly grasping at straws, and I tried to be as supportive as possible. She still insisted, "God can heal my husband. Please come and pray for him."

A deacon and I went to the hospital. The family gathered, I made my "no magic oil" speech, and then I prayed. I prayed a simple and direct prayer, "Lord, heal J. W. completely and immediately." I left out all the usual disclaimers about "if it's your will; if you desire," and so on. I simply prayed in faith, confessing that all other options were closed and asking God to intervene. Honestly, I didn't expect much to happen. I even told the deacon in the car on the way back home, "I doubt he will live through the night." In this case, I was the doubter—bemused at the possibility that healing might actually happen.

When my alarm sounded the next morning, I was surprised. I hadn't been called in the night with news of J. W.'s death. My first stop that morning was the hospital. I tapped on J. W.'s door and a strong male voice replied, "Come in." I slowly opened the door. To my surprise, J. W. was sitting up in bed, eating breakfast. "Hey, Pastor," he said. "If you don't mind, I'd like to keep working on breakfast. I woke up a couple of hours ago, and I'm really hungry. They finally brought me some food."

I stood there, dumbfounded—God had brought a man back from near death. God's power had been clearly demonstrated. That incident changed my perspective on healing and how to pray for it. It also convinced me of the reality of God's power.

In addition to experiencing God's power on a personal basis, leaders can also dream big about God's power at work through their church or organization. Veteran leaders, if beaten down by bitterness, can squelch those dreams. Soon after arriving at my first pastorate at the ripe old age of twenty-four, I shared lunch with a more experienced pastor. He asked about my ministry. In my youthful exuberance, I poured out my plans for reaching people and trusting God's power to build a strong church. His reply, "That's some vision. You'll get over it." I sat slack jawed—one of the few speechless moments of my life.

Rather than becoming more convinced of God's power to overcome impossible challenges, this pastor had allowed bitterness to rob him of confidence in God. Instead of encouraging words from an older pastor to a young pup, his comments made me feel embarrassed for being so vulnerable and enthusiastic. As I drove home, I prayed, "Lord, don't ever let that happen to me. Don't ever let me become a dream-crusher who doubts your power."

When you experience God's power as a younger leader, it not only meets the need in the moment but establishes a conviction about God's ability to intervene in the future. The best predictor of future behavior is past performance. Because you know God has worked in your life and ministry in the past, you know he will in the future. As the years roll by and the challenges become more and more impossible for you to meet in your own strength, have confidence in God's power, no matter how mountainous the problems seem to be.

QUESTIONS FOR REFLECTION

1. How has God demonstrated his power to you or through you?
2. Do you doubt God's power for your leadership? Why?
3. Has anyone tried to discourage you from trusting God in an impossible or improbable situation? How did you respond?

Lesson 7

TAKE RISKS

Matthew 14:22–33; Mark 6:45–52; John 6:16–21

 God's kingdom won't advance unless leaders take risks to obey God. Peter learned an important lesson about risk-taking one stormy night on the Sea of Galilee. Jesus had finished a demanding day of ministry, including feeding five thousand men (plus women and children) after a teaching session. He told the disciples to get in a boat and sail to the other side of the sea. He dismissed the crowd and went up on a mountain to pray. During the night, about 3:00 a.m., he decided to join the guys on the boat.

A storm had come up and was tossing the boat about in the waves. Jesus walked on the water through the storm and approached the boat. The disciples, already stressed by their circumstances, thought they were seeing a ghost. Before you poke fun at their reaction, think about it. If you fear being shipwrecked and see someone walking on the water toward you, what would you think? Believing they were seeing a ghost makes as much sense as thinking they were really seeing a person. After all, seeing someone or something walk on water through a storm would evoke all kinds of delusionary guesses about the identity of the apparition.

The disciples must have been shouting or otherwise communicating their fear because Jesus called out, "Have courage! It is I." Peter recognized

Jesus but wasn't fully convinced. He replied, "Lord, if it's You, command me to come to You on the water." Jesus replied, "Come."

Peter climbed out of the boat and started walking toward Jesus. How exciting those first few steps must have been. Wind howling, waves crashing, but Peter was walking on water toward Jesus. Imagine the exhilaration! Then Peter lost focus. He noticed the wind and waves and started to sink. Panicked, he called out for Jesus to save him. Jesus caught Peter and helped him back to the boat. When he was safe, Jesus said, "You of little faith. Why did you doubt?" Jesus focused on Peter's wavering faith. He cajoled Peter for losing focus in the midst of the storm.

There's no doubt that Peter's faith wavered. He lost his focus on Jesus and began to sink. He cried out, desperate to be delivered from a frightening situation. Many sermons have been preached on the symbolism of the ocean (life's challenges) and the importance of fixing your gaze on Jesus (not losing focus or faith). Those are appropriate insights—but only capture part of the meaning in these events.

One obvious fact in the story, however, is often overlooked: *Peter got out of the boat.* Twelve disciples saw the figure walking on the water. All of them probably heard Peter call out and discover it was Jesus. Any of the disciples could have responded to Jesus' invitation to meet him on the waves. Only Peter got out of the boat. While Jesus rebuked him for losing faith, at least he had faith to lose. The rest of the guys never left the boat. They were content to watch Peter climb out and walk to Jesus while they looked on from relative safety.

Peter learned this lesson that night: leaders take risks. They see Jesus walking where angels fear to tread and follow him there. They aren't content to sit safely, watching other people take risks. Leaders get out of the boat.

When my daughter Melody was a teenager, she attacked whatever sport she was playing. Particularly in basketball, she was a whirling dervish—a defensive specialist who usually guarded the best offensive player on the other team. Her "take no prisoners" style wasn't always appreciated by her opponents. In one game, she kept the other team's highest scoring player from scoring even a single point. In the middle of the fourth quarter, the other girl suddenly slammed the ball down and stomped off the court in tears. After that, to my wife's chagrin, my last words to my daughter before any game were, "Go make 'em cry!"

We often joked about my daughter's playing style in contrast to the "stand-around girls." They were the girls who stood around the gym, arms crossed, gossiping about other girls but never getting in the game. They were too cool to sweat, too self-absorbed to perform in front of other people, and too insecure to risk failure. Besides "go make 'em cry," my other watchword for my daughter was, "don't ever be one of the stand-around girls."

My daughter is now an emerging ministry leader who inspires me with her boldness and confidence. During college, she participated in a study-abroad program in Spain. She took the plunge and enrolled in courses like the history of Islam in Spanish rather than in English versions. Doing this was tough on her grade point average, but a much more direct path to Spanish fluency. While in Spain, to make friends and share the gospel, she joined a women's soccer team and worked in a women's prison ministry. Neither activity was part of her secular study-abroad program. She just took the initiative to find ways to expand God's kingdom.

The following year, she needed to serve an internship. Rather than take the safe route, she worked out a five-month internship in the Middle East. She served as a coach and mentor, helping to develop a women's basketball program. Her primary goal wasn't completing her education or getting some practical experience. Her goal was reinventing the internship assignment as a way to share the gospel in a difficult place by whatever means possible. Melody is definitely not one of the stand-around girls.

My most significant ministry leadership risk, as a younger leader, was planting a new church. We moved across the country, with three children under age five, from an established church, to start a church with four families in a middle school gymnasium. We had never lived in the part of the country where we relocated. My wife didn't even visit the area before we decided to move—our children were too young to make a trip for all of us practical.

When we made the decision to move to Oregon, some of our Christian friends thought we had lost our minds. We were leading a good church, had purchased a home, had a reasonable salary and benefits, were part of a great community in which to raise a family, and were in a place with a positive ministry future. While some questioned our sanity, we were never more certain of God's leading and never less concerned about the so-called risk. We had counted the cost and knew the risk of failure was reasonable given the possible reward—a new church in an underserved location.

Younger leaders have much less to lose by taking big risks than older leaders do. The challenge for emerging leaders is to risk wisely. The challenge for maturing leaders is to not become risk-averse as the stakes get higher. Remembering your riskier days, when youthful passion prompted bold choices, will help you avoid this problem. In order to have those memories as an older leader, however, you must take some risks when you are younger. Doing so both establishes a pattern of bold obedience and gives you firsthand experience with God's provision and protection. Our church-planting experience was seminal in establishing our life trajectory as leaders. We took a risk. God demonstrated his power in amazing ways. We have never been the same—as Christians and certainly not as leaders.

Get out of the boat. Take risks to follow Jesus. Build a personal portfolio of risk-taking experiences like my daughter has. Make bold decisions during your development years as a leader. Watch God protect you and reward you. As you accumulate those experiences, mentally catalog them as future reminders to keep taking risks—even when the stakes are higher. Once you learn the lessons of risk-taking obedience on a small scale, God will expand your opportunity and challenge you to take steps of faith you never imagined. Get out of the boat—and stay ready to get out of it again and again over the years.

QUESTIONS FOR REFLECTION

1. What is the biggest risk you have taken as a leader?
2. What are you facing in the future that will require a risk to expand God's kingdom?
3. What is your biggest obstacle to taking risks to advance the gospel?

Lesson 8

CONFESS THAT JESUS IS LORD

Matthew 16:13–20; Mark 8:27–30; Luke 9:18–20;
John 6:66–71

 While traveling to a new ministry location, Jesus asked his disciples what the crowds were saying about him. They replied that some thought he was John the Baptist, Elijah, Jeremiah, or another of the prophets returned to earth. This revealed two things about the prevailing opinion: People believed Jesus was both a great religious leader and a supernatural being. While both were true, something was missing in their assessment. So Jesus asked a more pointed question. "Who," he asked the Twelve, "do you say that I am?"

Peter answer boldly and succinctly. He replied, "You are the Messiah, the Son of the living God." This was the first time a disciple had voiced these claims about Jesus. Peter articulated the comprehensive truth about Jesus. He confessed him as the Messiah, the Christ, and the living Son of God. After many months of personal interaction, Peter announced this climactic conclusion: *Jesus is Lord.*

Jesus responded very positively to Peter's confession. He reminded Peter that these truths were more revealed than discovered; in a sense, he congratulated Peter on his spiritual acumen. Jesus told Peter that God had revealed his lordship to him. He then made Peter several promises. First, he promised Peter would be integral in establishing and building the church. Second, he promised Peter that the church would be sustained against the forces of hell. Third, he gave Peter the keys to the kingdom—useful for binding and loosing spiritual forces. Peter confessed Jesus as Lord and was rewarded with promises about his future usefulness in accomplishing God's purposes. His confession also resulted in new information about the longevity and durability of the church, as well as its centrality to God's purposes.

These were potent promises and breathtaking revelations. Their meaning has been debated for centuries. Was Peter promised the papacy? Does the church rest on Peter, his confession of Jesus, or on Jesus? What are the keys to the kingdom? What does it mean to bind and loose supernatural power?

While sorting all this out is very important, answering those questions isn't the purview of this book. For our purposes, remember the cogent question: "What did Peter learn about leadership in this situation?" The fundamental answer is: great leaders confess Jesus as Lord. When Peter's confession was made, Jesus responded with insight about himself, insight into following him, and promises about Peter's future usefulness. When we confess that Jesus is Lord, he does similar things for us. Confessing Jesus as Lord is foundational to leadership success.

Jesus pronounced Peter blessed as a result of his confession. When you acknowledge that Jesus is Lord, he delights in you and blesses you for recognizing his supremacy. God's eternal plan centers on gathering people into relationship with himself through his Son, Jesus. When you confess Jesus as Lord, you announce your submission to Jesus, your desire to be in relationship with God, and your recognition of your need for him. As a Christian leader, your relationship with God through Jesus is essential for success. Your confession of Jesus' lordship properly orients you to God through his Son. That's essential for leadership effectiveness.

When you confess Jesus as Lord, he stabilizes your status and stature before God. Peter was called "the rock" and promised integral participation in starting and sustaining the church. This story is the first time the word *church* is used in the Gospels. Peter's confession resulted in God revealing the idea of the church—which is later described as the consummation of God's purpose for the universe (Eph. 3:8–12). When you confess that Jesus is Lord, he uses you in ways previously unimagined. Consider Peter's surprise when he not only learned about the church, but his key role in launching and leading it. You may be similarly surprised at what God will reveal to you or use you to do after your confession of Jesus' lordship.

The longer I have been a leader, the more surprised I am that God uses me. The ways he has used me—to start a church and lead a seminary, for example—humble me. The older I get, the more aware I am of my sinfulness and leadership limitations. Yet, God uses me. As a younger leader, be encouraged. Your confession of Jesus as Lord opens your life to endless, surprising possibilities of God's work in you, through you, and around you.

When you confess that Jesus is Lord, he promises to work, not only in you, but *around* you in amazing ways. While Peter was promised a prominent role in the church, Jesus also reserved ultimate responsibility for the church's future to himself. Jesus said, "I will build My church." He said this to Peter in conjunction with his promises to use Peter in the process. When a leader confesses Jesus as Lord, Jesus somehow works more powerfully around that person—not just through him or her. Jesus surrounds a person submitted to his lordship with outpourings of his grace. Most Christian leaders are aware that God is at work around them in ways they can neither explain nor take credit for. Jesus delights in using leaders but also astounds and humbles us by accomplishing so much in spite of us.

When you confess Jesus as Lord, he also promises to work through you in powerful ways. He gave Peter the "keys of the kingdom." With those keys, Jesus told Peter "whatever you bind on earth is already bound in heaven, and whatever you loose on earth is already loosed in heaven." Those are remarkable promises. Jesus gave Peter unmatched authority and spiritual power. When a leader confesses that Jesus is Lord, he or she is then prepared to access the power Jesus has as Lord.

Jesus claimed all authority when he commissioned believers for service (Matt. 28:18–20). Jesus has all authority. All means all. When a leader assumes some authority—usually associated with a position or office—it's easy to forget the source from whence authority is derived. It doesn't come from a church or board or supervisor who grants it. All authority rests with Jesus, and while it may be shared through people and organizational structures in churches or ministries, it still originates with him. This means all leaders who exercise authority are accountable to Jesus for their actions. Only a person who has truly confessed Jesus as Lord—in full submission to his authority—is prepared to properly exercise the authority available in and through ministry leadership.

Emerging leaders often struggle with this issue. They careen between two extremes—limp passivity or absolute power. Passivity results from false humility and a failure to accept exercising authority as an appropriate aspect of leading people. Abuse of power comes from insecurity and the failure to respect the Source of all authority. Balance comes from gaining humility, and security by recognizing that all authority comes from Jesus. Younger leaders learn to exercise appropriate leadership authority. When they remember that Jesus is the Source of their authority, they don't shun it because of false humility or abuse it because of spiritual insecurity.

Your confession of Jesus as Lord prepares you to lead by giving you a good perspective on authority in leadership. Leaders have authority to make decisions, choose personnel, spend money, exercise discipline, and otherwise move forward the organization they are responsible to lead. Assuming that authority as if it somehow belongs to you or you are entitled to it is a recipe for disaster. Recognizing the authority of Jesus as Lord helps prevent misuse of authority in leadership relationships. It helps keep rogue ego in check—not that unchecked ego is much of a problem in leadership! When you live with a constant sense of Jesus' lordship, your leadership style will reflect that commitment.

Your confession of Jesus as Lord assures that he will be at work in, through, and around you. His lordship has ethical and behavioral implications for you personally. Your confession of Jesus as Lord means you reshape your life and leadership style to reflect your commitment to him. This personal transformation becomes foundational to your public role as a leader. Younger leaders experience the early phases of these changes; older leaders understand that the sharpening process never ends. Leading under lordship reflects submission to Jesus and results in appropriate authority for the role you have been assigned.

QUESTIONS FOR REFLECTION

1. Do you agree that Jesus is Lord?
2. How has your confession of Jesus as Lord affected your leadership style?
3. How does your submission to Jesus as Lord impact your use of authority in leadership?

Lesson 9

SUBMIT TO JESUS AS LORD

Matthew 16:21–28; Mark 8:31–9:1; Luke 9:21–27

 When Peter confessed Jesus' lordship, it was a profound moment—as if the scene should have been accompanied by crescendos of choral music supported by a full orchestra. Peter's confession and Jesus' response is a pinnacle event in the Gospels. Much of what preceded the moment was precursor to and preparatory for it. Immediately after Peter's confession, Jesus made clear and ominous predictions about his death. This interaction between Peter and Jesus was a point of demarcation. From this point forward, Jesus was focused on the cross. Peter, not so much.

Since Peter's confession was so significant, it would seem reasonable to assume it had immediate and permanent results on how he related to Jesus. Wrong. When you confessed Jesus as Lord, you probably intended the same long-lasting results, too, but have experienced a similar lack of consistency. Peter's confession of Jesus as Lord didn't result in permanent submission to his Lordship. Initial confession doesn't equal perpetual submission. It's difficult to actualize your confession of Jesus as Lord and particularize that decision into consistent action. Plainly put—it's hard to practice what you preach.

After affirming Peter and making the promises outlined in the previous chapter, Jesus told the disciples about his impending death. He told them he had to go to Jerusalem, that he'd suffer at the hands of the religious elite, die by their instigation, and then be resurrected from the dead. This must have been startling and troublesome news. Jesus was at the height of his popularity, and now he was talking about his death—an unjust death at that, resulting from persecution by religious leaders.

This was too much for Peter. He took Jesus aside and "began to rebuke Him." Yes, you read that right. Peter might have said something like, "Jesus, can I see you for a minute—over here in private." Then Peter rebuked him saying, "Oh no, Lord! This will never happen to You!"

Within minutes of confessing Jesus' lordship, Peter corrects Jesus—explaining to him what he can and cannot do, what he will and will not do. The most amazing word in Peter's corrective is "no." That word is even more interesting when juxtaposed with the next word in the sentence, "Lord." The irony would be comical if the stakes weren't so high. Peter told the Lord no. It's inconceivable that Peter misunderstood the meaning of the word "Lord." When someone is Lord, you cannot and do not tell them no. They are in charge. Your responsibility is submission, not rebuke. You obey with steely resolve; you don't resist with subtle arrogance. Telling the Lord no is a self-contradictory statement. If you confess Jesus as Lord, you forfeit the right to ever tell him no again. Whatever he says, goes. Your only response to Jesus is "Yes, Lord. Now what was the instruction?"

"You're not the boss of me," was the pithy way one preschooler announced her independence to my wife. She was at the age when a child experiences emerging self-identity. While her attitude was healthy in some aspects, she was also arrogantly exerting her independence. By rejecting the authority of her teacher, she was announcing that she was in charge. Most people mature past making this claim in such a blatant fashion. We are much more sophisticated in our resistance to Jesus' lordship.

Leaders must both confess Jesus' lordship and continually submit to Jesus as Lord. Leaders have amazing abilities to influence people, get projects done, assimilate information, and communicate with others. Leaders are gifted people, but without a clear understanding of Jesus as Lord, it's easy to become infatuated with those gifts. It's easy for leaders to develop delusions of grandeur, to become intoxicated by their success. When that happens, the leader loses effectiveness. He believes he is the center of the universe and capable of doing whatever it takes to advance the agenda.

There's a subtle, cyclical, downward spiraling trap of successful leadership. You face a big challenge. You confess your inadequacy and ask the Lord for his help. He empowers you to solve the problem. Success results. People praise you and celebrate your insight. You conclude (quietly, and perhaps a bit smugly) you really are a good leader who knows what you are doing. The next challenge arises. You take it on—trusting your proven wisdom and leadership skills to get the job done. Disaster happens and painful humiliation results. You may still confess Jesus as Lord in your doctrinal statement, but your submission to Jesus has evaporated. A leader's submission to the lordship of Christ is most often revealed in the midst of failure.

Peter followed a similar pattern. He confessed Jesus' lordship and was praised for his spiritual insight. He was promised spiritual power and assured of future usefulness. Then, almost immediately, pride in those accomplishments and recognitions produced spiritual arrogance so blatant that he called Jesus aside to correct him. When a leader assumes supremacy over Jesus, the rebuke will be immediate and potent.

Jesus told Peter, "Get behind Me, Satan! You are an offense to Me because you're not thinking about God's concerns, but man's." Wow! Just a few minutes before, Jesus had affirmed Peter for his spiritual sensitivity— "flesh and blood did not reveal this to you." Then he calls him Satan. That's quite a change, and a very forceful rebuke. When a leader takes matters into his or her own hands, assumes ultimate authority in a situation, or is so self-assured he tells Jesus what to do—rebuke is coming.

What's really happening when a leader does something like this? Jesus reveals the true problem with the second part of his rebuke of Peter. Jesus said, "You're not thinking about God's concerns, but man's." Peter had lost focus on advancing God's kingdom, God's way. His focus had shifted to accomplishing what he defined as God's agenda, his way. Peter made the mistake many leaders make. They redefine God's kingdom agenda in their terms. Then, with that redefinition in place, they attempt to orchestrate the next steps to fulfill their agenda. Jesus would have none of it from Peter—and he won't put up with it from you, either.

Emerging leaders must learn perpetual submission to Jesus as Lord. It's hard. You confess his lordship with every intention of living permanently under that confession. You soon learn how difficult it is to maintain submission to Jesus. You have offered yourself as a living sacrifice (Rom. 12:1), but the problem with a living sacrifice is, it keeps crawling off the altar.

Younger leaders may find that the first tastes of leadership success compound this problem. When things go well, it's easy to forget that Jesus empowered you, guided you, and enabled you through the process. People appreciate and praise you for your work. Subtly, often hidden behind pious platitudes, we find ourselves beginning to believe our own press clippings. We succumb to delusions of adequacy.

After living through the emerging-leader phase of life and coaching many others who are moving through that stage, I have a "bad news" conclusion: The cycle described above is inevitable. Everyone has to live through it and learn from it. Our innate sinfulness doesn't evaporate when we are called into a leadership role. Younger leaders have success, get full of themselves, experience rebuke (often in the form of a leadership failure), and learn fresh submission to Jesus. The challenge for younger leaders isn't to avoid this cycle; it's to recognize it and learn from it more quickly.

Emerging leaders must develop greater sensitivity to their propensity to advance their kingdom rather than God's. You must improve your capacity to sniff out nascent arrogance and nip it in the bud. You must learn to recognize signs of self-sufficiency and repent of them quickly. You must learn to experience spiritual victories and leadership successes without taking credit for them. As a younger leader, strive to shorten this cycle, not avoid it entirely.

Establishing this pattern of perpetual submission to Jesus is essential because—and here's some more bad news—the temptation of leadership success leading to self-sufficiency never relents. The cycle actually becomes worse as you become more skilled in leadership. As you accomplish more, the temptation to take the credit and think you know best how to lead God's people only increases. That's why establishing good patterns early in your leadership seasons is important. Learning early on that Jesus is Lord, submitting frequently to Jesus as Lord, repenting quickly when self-sufficiency replaces spiritual dependency, and truly advancing God's kingdom rather than your own establishes healthy patterns for a lifetime.

As an emerging leader, deeply ingrain these patterns now. They will serve you well as you navigate your future leadership challenges.

QUESTIONS FOR REFLECTION

1. How can you maintain perpetual submission to Jesus as Lord?
2. What are some signs that you are trusting your insight and advancing your kingdom rather than God's?
3. How has God used a leadership failure to break your cycle of self-sufficiency as a leader?

Lesson 10

DEVELOP HOLINESS

Matthew 15:1–20; Mark 7:1–23

 Pompous religious leaders aren't a modern phenomenon. They have been around a long time. Jesus was approached with a complaint from the scribes and Pharisees—the religious elite of their day. They asked Jesus, "Why do Your disciples break with the tradition of the elders? For they don't wash their hands when they eat." This question was based on a mutation of Jewish food preparation laws that morphed them from helpful guides reminding people of God's provision, into legalistic rituals supposedly producing spiritual purity. Hand-washing had been turned into a production number, an external badge of spiritual pride.

Jesus answered their question with a question of his own. He asked, "And why do you break God's commandments because of your tradition?" Jesus then summarized how the Pharisees and scribes ignored laws about caring for family members to further their careers in temple service. God expected children to honor their parents, to care for them with gifts to meet their needs as they aged. The religious rulers claimed that giving to the temple trumped family obligations. When asked for help, family members could say, "Sorry, the money has already been given at the temple. There's nothing left for you."

Jesus labeled the people who did this as hypocrites. He reminded them of Isaiah's prophecy about fallaciously honoring God with words—even words of worship—without meeting the needs of people in crisis. But this was only an example of a larger principle: external religious practices don't produce internal spiritual holiness.

To make sure his followers understood this principle, Jesus asked the crowd to draw closer. He told them, "It's not what goes into the mouth that defiles a man, but what comes out of the mouth, this defiles a man." The disciples were alarmed at Jesus' confrontational attitude toward the religious elite. They asked Jesus, "Do You know that the Pharisees took offense when they heard this statement?" Jesus knew the impact his comments would have. He fully intended to make his point, bluntly and publicly, to those who were creating religious systems to enrich themselves and facilitate personal promotion. Jesus counseled his followers, "Leave them alone! They are blind guides. And if the blind guide the blind, both will fall into a pit."

Peter witnessed this whole exchange, from the initial question to the final rejection of all that the scribes and Pharisees stood for. Typical of Peter, however, he had a follow-up request. Peter asked Jesus to "explain this parable to us." He was apparently referring to the parable of the blind guides—asking for further explanation of what seemed painfully obvious to everyone else.

Jesus' response has a hint of exasperation, "Are even you still lacking in understanding?" He then laid out the entire issue in plain terms. Jesus told Peter that what he touched and ate had little to do with personal holiness. The problem isn't what goes into the mouth, but what comes out. What comes out reveals a person's inner spiritual condition. Jesus listed several things that defile a person—"evil thoughts, murders, adulteries, sexual immoralities, thefts, false testimonies, blasphemies." These, Jesus concluded, "defile a man, but eating with unwashed hands does not defile a man."

Religious leaders who count on external practices to ensure holiness are modern scribes and Pharisees, futilely pursuing a legalistic means to personal purity. While hand-washing isn't a common example today, many other rules for religious people and special rules for religious leaders have been created. Sometimes, these expectations are forced on leaders. Other times, the leaders create the rules themselves. What does this look like today?

Some religious leaders are very particular about what they wear—dressing up or down or in whatever way that says, "Look at me." Others won't associate with people who smoke or drink or make questionable lifestyle choices. Some leaders also create rules for family members—children must always attend church, participate in every church activity, or otherwise model their parents' commitments. These rules further demonstrate the rightness of a leader's home life—they supposedly substantiate devotion in a clear way. Some leaders avoid certain forms of entertainment. Others insist that certain schools, degrees, or credentials are essential for genuine ministerial credibility. Some adopt particular theological systems, advocate certain doctrinal positions, or follow certain mentors to prove their devotion.

Some of these decisions are reasonable and can be helpful in spiritual development. Having personal convictions about related issues is appropriate. Problems arise, however, when leaders mistakenly substitute any of these standards for personal devotion. When a leader communicates that his or her practices create rather than reveal personal holiness, legalism results. Rather than demonstrating pure devotion to God, these external practices substitute religious activity for genuine commitment.

Leaders often struggle with these issues because they have become more concerned about their reputation than about purity before God. External practices can maintain a façade of devotion. They become a veneer, masking the empty reality that the absence of spiritual integrity denies the activity's real meaning. Going through the motions becomes more important than genuinely serving God. That the followers are fooled into thinking the leader has it all together is all that matters.

Jesus rejected this duplicity outright. He was always more concerned with a person's heart—their inner self. He was far more concerned with what comes out of a person, than what goes into a person. He was always more interested in the heart—why a person did something—the inner drive or motive—than in what a person did. Healthy leaders understand this important principle and focus on purifying their motives, clarifying what drives their actions, and doing things for the right reasons. These leaders refuse to do anything just to please other people or look good in front of others. They reject superficiality and strive for pure motives.

On one occasion, when he also rebuked hypocritical public displays, Jesus outlined a way to purify motives and ensure God's pleasure. He said, "When you pray, go into your private room, shut your door, and pray to your Father who is in secret. And your Father who sees in secret will reward you" (Matt. 6:6). One way to purify motives is to be sure you practice the spiritual disciplines like prayer in private as much or more than you do them in public. As a leader, much of your life is lived in front of others. That's natural. It comes with the territory. You are a model of the Christian faith, and people need to see you in action. But to overcome the temptation of equating public spiritual practices with personal spiritual devotion, you must simultaneously maintain a secret life of service and devotion.

As a younger leader, establish the practice of private prayer and Bible reading. Don't feel obligated to share everything you learn or experience in your time alone with God. Commit the insights to a journal, perhaps, but keep the information private. Emerging leaders should also establish the habit of giving secretly. Some money should be set aside for almsgiving (cash for people in need) or offerings given to ministries other than the one you lead. Another way to work in secret is to mentor a person one-on-one, quietly meeting their personal and practical needs. While you may some-day speak to thousands about their responsibility to minister to others, you must first model these practices by personally engaging individuals in ministry.

When you are engaged in personal devotion and secret service, God sees what you are doing and takes note. He promises to reward you. One of those rewards is the purifying effects that secret actions provide. When you do something in private, solely for God's pleasure, it sharpens your motives. When you do something similar in public—like praying, speaking, or giving—it will be an outgrowth of your private practices. When people praise you for what they see and receive, your awareness of serving out of the overflow of your relationship with God (rather than serving in order to prove or improve that relationship) will be an antidote for pride. Secret service has an inoculating effect on spiritual pride.

A leader's holiness is determined by what comes out of his or her life—authentic service motivated by pure devotion. What others see you do—if it's part of putting on a religious front—is fakery. Get past this charade early in your life of leadership.

Questions for Reflection

1. What legalistic practices in your context communicate spiritual devotion?

2. How does peer pressure help define the behavior of some Christian leaders?

3. What secret habits will you establish to help purify your motives as a leader?

Lesson 11

PRAY BOLDLY

Matthew 21:18–22; Mark 11:12–14, 20–26

Jesus cursing a fig tree was one of the most unusual events Peter observed during their time together. Jesus did it as an object lesson about the demise of the temple as the center of worship and the importance of prayer and faith in a proper relationship with God.

Jesus was on his way to Jerusalem. He was hungry and looked through the leaves of a fig tree for a meal—to no avail, since it wasn't the season for figs. Jesus then pronounced, "May no one ever eat fruit from you again!" The disciples heard him and probably wondered why Jesus would react so strongly to the absence of figs, given the time of year it was.

Jesus and the disciples continued their trip to Jerusalem, where Jesus confronted the money changers and others using the temple's grounds inappropriately. He reminded them that the temple was a house of prayer, not commerce. This upset the religious elite who were continually frustrated with Jesus' blunt assessment of their hypocrisy. No doubt the disciples were entranced by these events, wondering about their full meaning and the implications for the future of God's kingdom.

The next day, Jesus and his disciples passed by the cursed fig tree again. It was completely withered, down to the roots. Peter pointed out the

55

tree and reminded everyone it was the one Jesus had cursed. Jesus replied to Peter, "Have faith in God. I assure you: If anyone says to this mountain, 'Be lifted up and thrown into the sea,' and does not doubt in his heart, but believes that what he says will happen, it will be done for him. Therefore I tell you, all the things you pray and ask for—believe that you have received them, and you will have them."

That's a bold statement by Jesus. Many Christians struggle with the audacity of his promise related to prayer. The context was the Temple Mount—not just any mountain but the one connected with Jesus' activities of confronting the worship abuses the previous day. Jesus was telling Peter, as well as the other disciples, that what seemed impossible—overturning the temple as the center of worship—could and would happen soon. He was also challenging them to increase their faith in God as expressed through prayer. If the temple system could be replaced by a new way of relating to God (by faith in Jesus), then anything was possible with God.

This promise by Jesus has been misinterpreted by some to equate "working up faith" with getting answers to your prayers. There is a clear connection between faith and prayer, but trying to pump up your faith to guarantee that God will answer your prayers isn't what Jesus was teaching. These instructions from Jesus must be understood in the context of the story (the trip to the Temple), as well as his many other instructions about prayer. In this case, Jesus was challenging his disciples to greater faith in God. He wanted them to trust God in more significant ways than they'd previously imagined. Jesus challenged Peter to trust God for bigger changes and believe God for strength to overcome bigger challenges. Jesus challenged the disciples to pray bigger prayers.

Jesus has a way of shaping life to create "fig-tree" experiences to expand your vision. When I was in college, our church sponsored a prayer conference led by a man named Don Miller. He was, at that time, a well-known speaker who specialized in four-day conferences designed to significantly improve a church's commitment to prayer. In one of his sessions, asked this question: "What are you praying for that seems impossible?"

He asked us to write our answer on a note card. My mind raced to think about my greatest need. I wrote it on the card. I needed $500 to pay my tuition for the following semester. That seemed like a huge amount of money at the time. I thought, "If he asks us to read our cards, the church will really be impressed by my faith." It's embarrassing to admit, but I was quite proud of what I had written. I was sure no one else could possibly ask for anything as bold as my request for $500.

Then Miller thundered, "What are you asking for that seems impossible? I am asking God to reveal the cure to all cancer in my lifetime!" I was shocked. Reveal the cure for all cancer in his lifetime? That didn't *seem* impossible, that was impossible. But wasn't that the point? I was humbled and humiliated. I was humbled by the boldness of Miller's request. I was humiliated at my pride in my pathetic request. I quietly tore up my card and spent the next few minutes praying—not for $500, but repenting of my pride and asking God to teach me what it really means to pray boldly.

About twenty years after that prayer conference, I was diagnosed with thyroid cancer. While there was risk involved in the surgery, I was delighted to learn this kind of cancer is curable in most cases. When my doctor explained this to me, my thoughts went back to Miller's request. Had the cure been revealed in the intervening twenty years? Was my future health directly tied to Miller's request? Was his prayer answered by God's grace extending to and through some smart researcher? It was a sobering thought. God is revealing the cures for cancer, at least in part to one man's audacious asking.

This story has motivated me to pray bigger prayers. For example, becoming friends with a prominent athlete (also well-known for his carousing) motivated me to pray for his salvation. It seemed impossible. He was too busy chasing women, boozing it up, and enjoying the pleasures his wealth and notoriety provided. Then, one day, he told me he had committed his life to Jesus. What seemed impossible actually happened.

When we planted a church, we prayed for many people to come to faith in Jesus. We asked for money to meet our needs. We asked for land to build a campus. We asked for leaders to continually expand our organization. When the church was just a few families, small enough to meet in a living room, these things seemed impossible. But we prayed; God answered; and miracles ensued. A large, growing, healthy church resulted.

We wanted to start a new degree program at our school. We looked at the finances, and it was clear we didn't have the money to fund the expansion. We prayed for seven years for the resources to begin the program. We approached donors whom we thought might be interested, to no avail. One day, out of the blue, a person who had no idea we had this dream asked one of our leaders if we had ever considered starting this particular program.

When she learned we had, she asked how much it would cost—and wrote a six-figure check to get it done. We had prayed and done all we could by asking interested people for gifts. God had a different plan and a different timetable. Amazingly, within a few months after this initial gift, the seminary received a seven-figure endowment gift designated for the same degree program. That gift had been committed in an estate plan more than a decade before we started the program. God answered our prayer and then overwhelmed us with two gifts to guarantee the program's success for years to come.

Emerging leaders are often idealistic, see incredible needs, and passionately want to do something about them. Unfortunately, these leaders are sometimes negatively influenced by veteran leaders who are jaded about ministry. As mentioned previously, that was my experience when an older pastor projected his discouragement onto my future plans. Your challenge as a younger leader is to reject naysayers and boldly ask God for the impossible. The greatest church-planting movements haven't yet been started. The best evangelistic methods haven't yet been discovered. The most effective new churches aren't yet planted. The schools, hospitals, relief ministries, and mission boards needed to reach the world with the gospel haven't yet been organized. God is raising up a visionary generation to change the world. You are part of this generation. Ask big and expect God to do what seems impossible.

QUESTIONS FOR REFLECTION

1. Have you had a fig-tree experience to teach you about God's ability to do the impossible? Describe it.
2. What are you praying for right now that seems impossible?
3. How will you keep naysayers from robbing you of vision for the future?

FORGIVE OTHERS

Matthew 18:21–35

 After hearing Jesus' teaching about restoring sinful brothers, Peter asked Jesus an important question about forgiveness. It was a direct question, with a hint of Peter's willingness to go the extra mile (as he understood it) to demonstrate God's grace toward others. Peter asked, "Lord, how many times could my brother sin against me and I forgive him? As many as seven times?"

Seven is an interesting number. It often communicates fullness or completeness—like the seven days of creation or the seven days of the week. Since the Sabbath is every seventh day, seven is also equated with worship or godliness. Rabbinic law required forgiveness be granted three times. Peter's offer reflected his growing understanding of God's grace, learned by watching Jesus relate compassionately to people in need. He probably considered his offer of forgiving seven times to be somewhat magnanimous in light of the rabbinic standard and Jesus' example.

The Lord had a different perspective. He told Peter to forgive seventy times seven times! One person tried to convince me this meant we are supposed to forgive 490 times, but no more. He missed the point. Jesus multiplied Peter's generous offer to forgive seven times to demonstrate the extravagant nature of God's forgiveness. He forgives lavishly and expects us to extend forgiveness to others in a similar way. Jesus then followed his startling statement about extravagant forgiveness with a parable further proving his point.

In the parable, a king wanted to settle accounts with his servants. He called in a servant who owed ten thousand talents. The servant was unable to pay, so the king ordered that his family and possessions be sold to satisfy what he owed. The servant begged for more time, promising to pay off the debt in full. The king had compassion on him and forgave the debt.

The servant then went looking for people who owed him money. He found a fellow slave who owed him a hundred talents and demanded payment, grabbing and choking him in the process. When the second servant begged for additional time to repay the debt, the first servant refused and had him tossed into prison. The other servants saw what happened and reported it to the king, who was livid. He called in the first servant, rebuked him for his duplicity, and had him put in prison. Jesus concluded, "So My heavenly Father will also do to you if each of you does not forgive his brother from his heart."

Jesus made this principle clear: extravagant forgiveness prompts extravagant forgiveness. Just as God has forgiven you, you must learn to forgive others. Jesus made a special effort to teach Peter this principle. Why? Because every emerging leader must learn to forgive others. It's a survival skill necessary for leadership effectiveness. Later in their relationship, Peter would fail Jesus and personally experience the profound truth taught by this parable. Leaders fail people who are close to them; they are hurt by those they serve; and they are sometimes unjustly wronged by others. Learning to forgive is essential in every situation.

As you prepare to assume leadership responsibilities, you must grant forgiveness for wounds inflicted in your past. Many emerging leaders didn't grow up in committed Christian families or healthy churches. They have baggage from past relationships—some things they caused and some that were inflicted on them. Some younger leaders have been victims of sexual sin—abuse, incest, date rape, etc. Others have been emotionally scarred by absentee parents or divorce. Some have dealt with the opposite extreme— parents who placed unrealistic demands on them. Sadly, some younger leaders have emerged from dysfunctional churches where leaders abused their members and weren't held accountable for their actions. Watching rogue members abuse ministry leaders also scares younger leaders.

One young believer was reluctant to respond to God's call to ministry leadership. His primary reason was the abuse his father had endured as a pastor. He was unwilling to subject himself or his future family to similar treatment. Another emerging leader imported into his early leadership roles the coping mechanism of perfectionism (learned from growing up in an alcoholic family). This produced great frustration and feelings of failure when early ministry efforts weren't perfect. Another novice leader had been abandoned by a serious boyfriend, which left her unable to trust others. That is a real problem when building ministry relationships.

The solution to all these situations was forgiveness. The first person had to forgive the church members who abused his father. The second had to forgive his father for the impact of his addiction. The third had to forgive the guy who jilted her. In all three cases, forgiveness was the key to overcoming the detrimental impact these debilitating relationships had on these up-and-coming leaders. Forgiving others sets you free from the bad situations of your past that would otherwise limit your present and future effectiveness in developing leadership relationships.

Leaders must also learn to forgive the difficult people they encounter early in their emerging leadership roles. The younger you are, the more mistakes you will make. With their perfect hindsight, some people delight in pointing out your shortcomings and telling you how to do better next time. Younger leaders are the most vulnerable members of the leadership herd. They are often assailed by critics. It probably seems to many younger leaders that they attract persistent critics—sharks who smell blood in the water and move in quickly for the kill. Skilled critics have an innate sense of when others are vulnerable, and they know just how to attack them. Younger leaders often attract abusive critics.

Learning to handle critics requires relational skill and emotional dexterity. Some critics must be confronted; some ignored. Some are right, and you need to change at the point of criticism. All must be endured. No matter which category describes the criticism, it always hurts. If not properly treated, those wounds can fester into emotional sores that will poison leadership relationships and negate leadership influence. The healing balm for those wounds is forgiveness—apply it lavishly and often.

Forgiving others the way God has forgiven you is a spiritual challenge. You must forgive others when they have sinned against you. You must forgive others whether they ask for it or not. You must forgive quickly, before a root of bitterness is sown in your spirit. You must forgive repeatedly—remember seventy times seven! You must forgive people when revenge would be so much sweeter. And, finally, you must forgive the people who disappoint you—like fellow Christians who ought to be your friends and supporters.

All this presupposes a basic reality—you have been forgiven by God, and you have fully accepted his forgiveness. Leaders, like other believers, sometimes struggle in accepting God's forgiveness for their past sins. You may have rebellion, moral failure, or an ethical lapse in your background. You carry the guilt of your sin, and it distorts your view of yourself and your leadership potential. If you have asked God to forgive your past sins, he has forgiven you. Accept that reality. Live released from false guilt—the condemnation Satan heaps on as you remember your past sins. You may never forget what you have done, but you must learn to remember it as forgiven.

An unforgiven sin in your past is like a caged lion. Given any opportunity, it will escape and ravenously destroy everything it can reach. A forgiven sin, on the other hand, is like a toothless lion. It's still alive in your memory, but it has lost the capacity to take a bite out of you every time you remember it. God will forgive any sin in your past. As an emerging leader, come clean before him. Get past sin out in the open. Confess what you have done. Repent. Ask God for forgiveness and receive the extravagant forgiveness he grants. No sin is outside the bounds of what God can and will forgive. Whatever guilt you are carrying can be alleviated by God's forgiveness.

A clean conscience is essential for effective leadership. Being forgiven is a precursor to forgiving others. The absence of duplicity and hidden relational agendas means you can lead people without having to hide anything. You can be transparent about your past, knowing God has forgiven you. You can also be transparent with your followers, asking forgiveness, forgiving them, and moving forward to fulfill your leadership responsibility among them.

QUESTIONS FOR REFLECTION

1. What wound from your past needs to be healed through forgiveness?
2. Who are the hardest people for you to forgive? Why?
3. What is the most difficult aspect of God's forgiveness for you to accept? What will you do to change in this area?

Lesson 13

LIVE URGENTLY

Matthew 24:36–51; Luke 12:35–48

 Jesus is coming again. He may come at any moment. Is this conviction reflected in how you live and lead others? Jesus communicated urgency about his second coming while he was with his disciples. He wanted them—and us—to know he wouldn't always be physically present, but he would return to earth at some time in the future. During the interim, he wants his followers to live with expectancy and urgency based on that reality.

A huge crowd had gathered to hear Jesus. His message that day started with a focus on making good choices for healthy living around the theme of trusting God for daily needs. Soon he shifted his focus to living for the future and allowing convictions about the future to control and motivate daily choices. As usual, Jesus taught these lessons in parables.

Jesus first compared his followers to servants waiting for their master to return from a wedding banquet. Jesus described a good servant as one who was awake, ready to unlock the door and welcome his master home whenever he might appear. This alert servant would be blessed with both the master's favor and service in return. Jesus then reinforced this lesson with a second, similar parable. He likened his followers to a homeowner who had been burglarized. If the homeowner had known when the thief was coming, he would have taken steps to prevent the intrusion. Jesus concluded these two parables by challenging the crowd, "You also must be ready, because the Son of Man is coming at an hour you do not expect."

Peter then asked a pertinent question about the scope of the application of this parable. He asked the Lord, "Are You telling this parable to us or to everyone?" Although that seems like a "yes" or "no" type question, Jesus answered with yet another parable. By using another story, he completed a triad of word pictures designed to solidify this lesson in the minds of the disciples . . . and future leaders like you.

In the third parable, Jesus described a wise master who singled out a household servant to manage his affairs while he was away. The trusted servant would make sure the other servants were fed and cared for properly, and would manage them to fulfill the master's business. One primary quality of the trusted servant was faithfulness when the master was absent. But even that servant could be tempted during the master's prolonged absence. Suppose, Jesus postulated, the faithful servant doubted the master's return and became a negligent manager. What if he beat the other slaves, threw lavish parties, and got drunk. What would happen when the master returned?

When the master discovered the servant's irresponsibility and unfaithfulness, he would be judged severely—"cut . . . to pieces" and "severely beaten." (Keep in mind that this is a parable with colorful language used to make a point, not a description of an actual beating and dismembering. Jesus was emphasizing dire consequences, not advocating torture for unfaithful servants.) He then balanced that statement with this reminder: a servant who made these mistakes inadvertently would receive lesser consequences—he would be "beaten lightly."

After emphasizing these general outcomes, Jesus then sharpened his application of the parable to Peter and the disciples. While acknowledging the universal application of the parable, he answered Peter's question by reminding his leaders-in-training that they had a higher level of accountability because of their privileges and responsibilities.

Jesus told Peter, "Much will be required of everyone who has been given much. And even more will be expected of the one who has been entrusted with more." While everyone is expected to prepare for Jesus' return, leaders bear a greater responsibility than other believers. Leaders are responsible to model, teach, and motivate other believers to stay ready.

We are responsible to keep the parabolic "kingdom house" in order while waiting for the Master's return. We are represented by the more highly accountable servants in the story, those who may be "severely beaten," not the other servants who "did not know" and will only be "beaten lightly." Again, this is hyperbolic language in a parable—not a literal warning. The force of the hyperbole, however, is significant. Jesus expects his followers to live urgently, making lifestyle choices in light of his possible return. Further, Jesus expects kingdom leaders to model urgency and encourage others to follow their example. When we fail to do this, the consequences will be severe—both for us and, sadly, for our followers.

As a younger leader, it can be difficult to balance planning for the future with living for the present. For example, should you have a retirement fund? Should you exercise so you can live healthier and longer? Should you save for your children's education? Should you even have children, given the possibly short time until Jesus returns? Should you quit school and just start telling people about Jesus? Does living urgently in light of the Second Coming mean you only live in the moment? These are tough questions with complex answers. There are two principles, however, to guide you as you sort out the solutions.

First, make the big decisions in life in light of Jesus' return. Choosing your spouse and vocation for example, are two types of big decisions. If you are serious about living your life in light of Jesus' return, you cannot counteract that desire by marrying someone—even a Christian—who has different life goals. If your prospective spouse is materialistic, you won't be able to live frugally and give generously to ministry projects. If he or she needs to live close to family, you can't answer a call to take the gospel to billions who have never heard of Jesus. If you choose to be consumed by your vocation, you will find yourself chasing the American dream rather than living for the kingdom of God. If you are a ministry leader who chooses ministry leadership as a career rather than a calling, you will be more focused on success now rather than eternal results. Make the big decisions in life by asking, "Does this decision reflect my commitment to living as if Jesus will return soon?"

Second, make priority decisions balanced by the imminence (sure to happen, but uncertain of the time) of Jesus' return. For example, save *some* money for retirement—but not toward the goal of amassing wealth. Save to take care of yourself so you won't be a burden on others who need to spend their time and money on kingdom advance, not taking care of you. Save for retirement so you can remain a self-funded kingdom worker when you are no longer able to work for others. Prioritize spending *most* of your current resources to immediately advance God's kingdom agenda but save *some* for the same purpose in the future.

The same principle applies to areas like education and exercise. Your emphasis should be on *now*, while investing some effort in the future. As an emerging leader, you need some schooling, but only that which is required to fulfill your ministry or life assignment. Getting another degree is often more about your ego than God's kingdom. Get the education you really need and then get busy. The same is true for exercise. Caring for your body and not abusing yourself into burnout makes you more effective now and keeps you from being a burden to others in the future. Appropriate exercise is important; striving for eternal youth or being inappropriately fixated on appearance contradicts eternal values and must be avoided.

Common wisdom on these issues advocates "all things in moderation." That's not what I'm describing. "All things in proper perspective" would be closer to the biblical philosophy underlying these principles. Proper perspective means acknowledging the demands of daily life while making choices about them in light of Jesus' certain return. Proper perspective means devoting appropriate resources and energy to these issues, with the majority devoted to the present and some invested in the future. Urgency is demonstrated by balanced choices that assure the long-range application of your conviction that Jesus is coming again. It is not just living in the moment.

Leaders are expected to model these principles over a lifetime. Younger leaders must be careful to establish these patterns early, avoiding entanglements that will undermine future effectiveness. Establish Jesus' imminent return as a factor in your decision-making now before other life demands clutter your agenda. Recognize and accept your responsibility to model these choices for your followers. Jesus is coming again—learn to live in light of that reality.

QUESTIONS FOR REFLECTION

1. Do you believe Jesus will come again soon? Why?
2. Why is it important for leaders to be vigilant about decision-making based on the conviction that Jesus will return soon?
3. What decisions are you currently facing that need to be made in light of Jesus' imminent return? What will you do?

Lesson 14

LIVE FOR ETERNAL REWARDS

Matthew 19:16–30; Mark 10:17–31; Luke 18:18–30

 Everyone likes rewards. Employee recognitions, credit card offers, frequent flyer programs, and loyalty cards at department stores all tap into this aspect of human nature. We like to know our efforts are noticed and our business is appreciated. As a Christian leader, you aren't exempt from this desire to be rewarded. While you may resist recognition to avoid pride and practice humility, the fact you are resisting something proves it's real. You have a natural desire to be rewarded when you do something right.

Peter was no different. After a poignant exchange between Jesus and a wealthy young man raised the issues of eternal life and rewards for kingdom living, Peter asked Jesus a question that revealed how important this issue was to him. Jesus' response—what he said and how he said it—were helpful for Peter and will be encouraging to you.

A man—traditionally known as the rich young ruler—approached Jesus and asked him about obtaining eternal life. The man called Jesus "good teacher," but Jesus took issue, reminding him only God was good. He then challenged the young man to keep all the commandments. This seemed like good news to this morally upright fellow. He asked Jesus, "Which ones?" and Jesus listed the most prominent commandments. The young ruler was delighted, for he had successfully kept the commandments Jesus mentioned. Then Jesus added another dimension when he said, "Go, sell your belongings and give to the poor, and you will have treasure in heaven. Then come, follow Me." The rich young ruler's response was tragic. He walked away from Jesus, grieving, because he had many possessions. Nevertheless, he still walked away.

Jesus then turned to the disciples and reminded them how difficult it was for a rich person to enter the kingdom of God. He used an illustration of a camel trying to go through the eye of a needle to underscore his point about the difficulty of a wealthy person surrendering to Jesus' lordship.

The disciples were astonished and asked, "Then who can be saved?" Jesus told them, "with God all things are possible." Peter had listened to the dialogue between Jesus and the ruler, as well as heard the disciples' question. He was, quite possibly, reflecting on his decision to leave behind a commercial fishing business to follow Jesus. He had given up his company, a steady source of income, and the respected role of being a provider for his community. He'd left home and family to follow Jesus. While he might not have been considered rich, he was definitely not poor. He had given up quite a bit to follow Jesus. In that context, Peter's question is legitimate—not a whiney question from someone who doubts his decision but an honest question about the future. Peter said to Jesus, "Look, we have left everything and followed You. So what will there be for us?"

The appropriateness of the question and the attitude with which it was asked are significant. Their legitimacy is revealed by what Jesus did *not* say in response. Jesus didn't rebuke Peter. We know from other incidents Jesus wasn't averse to confronting and correcting Peter. This time he didn't chide him for pride, lack of faith, or selfishness. Jesus simply answered the question. Jesus' noncritical, nonjudgmental response is significant. He understands the sacrifices that leaders make to serve him and he wants them to understand the rewards he gives.

The tone and legitimacy of the question is further established by the first words in Jesus' answer. "I assure you," he says. Not, "I rebuke you" or "I can't believe you are asking me that." Jesus responded to Peter's summary of the sacrifices he had made by assuring him that proper notice had been taken and meaningful rewards would follow. Jesus then summarized the nature of the rewards for leaders who sacrifice to serve him.

Jesus promised Peter eternal recognition and leadership responsibilities. He promised Peter that he would be enthroned eternally with him. While this is figurative language, what it symbolizes is significant. Leaders who sacrifice for Jesus will rule with him eternally. What this means, fully, is a mystery. But it sounds awesome! Heaven won't be a place for passive harp playing. It will somehow involve continued service for and with Jesus. The first eternal reward that leaders are promised is the joy of eternal leadership. Leaders thrive on leading. Getting to do it for eternity is a blessing not a burden.

Jesus then promised Peter generous provision in this life to replace whatever had been sacrificed for kingdom service. He said, "Everyone who has left houses, brothers or sisters, father or mother, children, or fields" will receive "100 times more." There are three categories of sacrifice enumerated by Jesus: houses (security of a home/homeland), family (brothers, sisters, parents, children), and vocation/career (fields). Jesus assured Peter that, since he had given up home, family, and career, God would take note and reward him.

Finally, Jesus promised Peter he would "inherit eternal life" in addition to the aforementioned blessings. This did not mean he didn't already, as a believer, have eternal life. It meant he would get rewards in this life and the next. Eternal life on top of the blessings provided in this life. The Gospel of Mark underscores these blessings in the midst of persecutions that come with leadership. Even in the most trying circumstances, these rewards—now and later—will be provided to kingdom leaders.

Emerging leaders face the temptation of trying to achieve temporal rewards. You may have peers in other careers making more money than you. They have nicer cars and houses, eat at the best restaurants, take expensive vacations, and wear designer clothes. You shop at Goodwill, use food stamps to make it through seminary, and watch the Travel Channel. Your friends will live close to their parents and grandparents. You will lead in isolated places where you are the only Christian for miles. Your children will grow up seeing their grandparents once a year, if that often. Yet you are willing to make those sacrifices to advance God's kingdom. Rest assured, Jesus notices and promises rewards.

Jesus promises to reward you in this life. He does this by giving you special provision, from time to time, to make life more enjoyable. Over the years, we have been given clothes, money to travel, furniture, and other practical items. God also gives special relationships to replace those diminished through kingdom service. Our family, for example, has lived far from grandparents and other supportive family members. We have been grateful for surrogate grandparents God has provided. We have also developed relationships with fellow believers who have become like family and have met our deepest needs for familial connections. We have found a new homeland in our ministry setting on the West Coast which has become more precious to us than where we originally lived. God has given us provision, relationships, and stability greater than anything we could have imagined. We tried to sacrifice to follow God's plan for our lives, but the rewards have been so generous we really can't define what we have done as a sacrifice.

Jesus also promises to reward you in eternity. Certainly, the primary reward is being with Jesus forever. Another reward is serving Jesus and serving with Jesus forever. While the nature of this service isn't really clarified in the Bible, just its possibility, no matter how it's defined, is reward enough. Another eternal reward will be seeing the results of your leadership in heaven. People will be there who committed themselves to Jesus as Lord and Savior through your influence. Some will be people you will recognize. Others will be there because of money you gave, other leaders you trained, or some other indirect means of extending your influence. We will gain a new perspective in heaven of the true cause and effect of human initiative. My hunch is that we will be quite surprised by the full impact of our leadership efforts.

Leaders want rewards for their service. That's human nature. Jesus knows your need and instead of rebuking you, he assures you that he will reward you. When you prioritize his kingdom, he notices. He sees your sacrifices and rewards you appropriately. As a younger leader, have faith to set aside pursuit of temporary rewards and trust Jesus for the eternal kind.

QUESTIONS FOR REFLECTION

1. How do you feel when peers receive rewards like promotions, salary raises, or other financial perks? Why?
2. Do you struggle with the pain of distant relationships because of kingdom leadership responsibilities? How do you manage that sense of loss?
3. Have you already experienced some rewards for your leadership sacrifices? What do these portend for your future?

Lesson 15

LEAD FROM THE FUTURE

Mark 13:1–37

 Jesus said some things that must have seemed implausible, even ridiculous, when the disciples first heard them. On the way out of the temple complex one day, Jesus said, "Do you see these great buildings? Not one stone will be left here on another that will not be thrown down!" Considering the size (some stones as big as boxcars), sacred stability, and longevity of the temple, it was inconceivable that Jesus could really mean what he said.

Peter, James, John, and Andrew thought this through while walking across the Kidron Valley to the Mount of Olives. When they arrived, they asked Jesus two questions about his audacious prediction about the temple. They asked, "Tell us, when will these things happen? And what will be the sign when all these things are about to take place?"

Jesus' answer to those questions combined insights about two important future events—the physical destruction of the temple (which happened in AD 70) and the cataclysmic events associated with Jesus' second coming. Sorting out those issues is a fascinating study of first-century history and still-to-come eschatological events that are best left for another book. Our question centers on what Jesus taught Peter about leadership, not details about future events. The key lesson for Peter was to anticipate the future by understanding the times. Leaders must lead from the future, making decisions from that perspective rather than striving for perpetual preservation of their current status or past successes.

Leaders must understand the times in which they live and work. They may have nostalgia for perceived better days or dream of easier locations—but not if they want to effectively lead in the here and now. All leaders face the temptation of preserving their era, not realizing contexts continue to change throughout our lifetime. For example, as younger leaders, my generation would often say, "It's not the 1950s any longer" when calling for change in the church. After all, it was the 1980s—thirty years had passed, and it was time to come up to date. My generation wanted to update the church, but now we seem determined to preserve the 1980s. These days, it would be appropriate to call for change by saying, "It's not the 1980s any longer." Think about it—we are now thirty years past the 1980s—just like my generation was thirty years past the 1950s.

Every generation of leaders faces the challenge of updating churches or ministry organizations. We must keep up-to-date with contemporary experience. We implement new methods and enjoy the successes they produce. Soon, however, they are no longer new methods, but preserving them is comfortable and still somewhat effective. Resisting this temptation is a significant leadership challenge. We must periodically reinvent our ministries by incorporating changing methodologies required for continued effectiveness. We must learn to lead from the future—looking ahead and continually changing to meet coming realities.

This is particularly important for successful churches or ministries. Past or present success is a prime inhibitor of change. It's hard to convince people to fix what isn't broken. Religious commitments often involve emotional attachments to people, places, and/or programs. We become comfortable and equate those relationships with spiritual vitality. These connections make change very difficult. Nevertheless, it is a primary responsibility of leaders to look into the future and initiate the changes necessary to move an organization successfully forward.

Sometimes, the needed changes you see on the horizon aren't mere adjustments—they are game changers. When Jesus told Peter the temple would be destroyed, imagine how he might have received the news. First, shock. Then, musing how it might happen. Finally, realization of what it would mean and how different the future of worship would be. These events would conclusively end a centuries-old way of doing things. The gravity of the situation may have been a bit unnerving as Peter realized the full impact of what he was learning.

But there was more: Jesus predicted another coming event with profound ramifications for future ministry leadership. He predicted his return and concomitant events bringing the world as we know it to an end. As Peter heard those predictions, he must have wondered about their full meaning. When would Jesus return? How long would it be until it happened? What should be done in the meantime? How should this message be communicated? Would anyone believe it to be true?

Peter was challenged to understand the times and anticipate future trends as revealed by current events. He had a remarkable advantage on the rest of us. Jesus explained these things to him personally and directly. There could be no doubt of the importance of this information and its application to future ministry decisions. A new way of relating to God was dawning since the temple was coming down. The kingdom of God on earth now had a shelf life with a definite end in view since Jesus was coming again. Peter was expected to lead in light of these future realities.

Younger leaders may struggle to anticipate the future and lead from that perspective. Part of the reason is that Jesus won't give you the kind of detailed report he gave Peter. Nevertheless, you are responsible to understand the times you live in, the future you are moving toward, and how to lead in light of that information. How can you improve your capacity to anticipate the future by more accurately understanding current events? How can you understand the times? How can you lead in light of the ultimate future reality—the return of Jesus?

First, discover what the Bible says about the future. The Bible describes the erosion of good and the rise of evil as the world's future trajectory. It also promises the church will survive the worst the world throws at it. Biblical prophecies describe diminished fear of God and increased lawlessness as time passes. These are important predictions and leaders are responsible to make plans and decisions accordingly.

Second, learn what the Bible says about present world conditions and how they relate to future events. Some of what Jesus said to the disciples described the future, but now it sounds a lot like our present. When the Bible predicts future apostasy, immorality, and idolatry—it speaks of the future the original recipients could anticipate. Their future sounds a lot like today's world. Make leadership decisions based on those realities.

Third, learn what insightful people are predicting about the future. Futurists study trends in disparate fields and merge the information to postulate coming realities. Beware of people who claim they can predict the future; take seriously people who studiously anticipate the future. One smacks of arrogance; the other of wisdom. Beware also the humanistic tendency to believe that humans, by their own ingenuity, will continue to improve world conditions. Governments and companies pay millions for information to shape current decisions based on assumptions about the future. Pay attention to similar information and use it wisely while recognizing its humanistic limitations.

Fourth, consider the insights of mature Christian leaders who have perspective that younger leaders don't yet have. Veteran leaders are often able to distinguish between fads and trends and provide insightful counsel accordingly. This doesn't necessarily mean experienced leaders can predict the future. It means they can discern what current events reveal about future realities. Wise leaders make decisions accordingly.

Finally, ask God for insight about the future. God will answer this prayer—by spiritual promptings, by flashes of insight from his Word, through information from cultural observers, and from the counsel of wiser leaders. God knows your leadership demands require decisions about the future. He isn't playing cat and mouse, trying to frustrate or trick you. Ask him for insight and trust that he will give it.

Peter knew that the destruction of the temple would have significant implications for how people related to God in the future. As Jesus described events related to his return, Peter must have also mulled their significance for his future kingdom leadership. As you develop your leadership perspective, learn to lead from the future. Be aware of current events—the signs of the times—and what they reveal about future ministry conditions in your setting. Be more aware of future realities, learn to anticipate what is just over the horizon, and plan how your church or ministry organization will respond. The best leaders are ahead of the curve; they are not constantly trying to catch up. Learn to lead from the future.

QUESTIONS FOR REFLECTION

1. What are the "signs of the times" in your setting that should inform your leadership decisions?

2. What is one key aspect of the future that your church or organization needs to consider more carefully as it plans for the days ahead?

3. Why is it easier when things are going well to preserve the status quo and more difficult to make changes to assure future effectiveness?

SERVE HUMBLY

John 13:1–20

Jesus and the disciples gathered just before the Passover for their evening meal. During the meal, Jesus quietly slipped away from his place at the table, removed his robe, tied a towel around his waist, and poured a basin of water. The disciples, as was the custom, were reclining at the table. This meant they were lying prone, propped by an elbow, facing inward with their feet extending away from the table. In this position, diners could have their feet washed while they ate. This was menial work assigned to the lowliest servants. Touching feet was taboo; washing them even worse.

The Twelve appeared oblivious to their feet being washed. Why pay attention, when no one worth acknowledging would be doing it? Jesus worked his way down the line unnoticed, until he came to Peter who looked down and asked, "Lord, are You going to wash my feet?" Jesus answered, "What I'm doing you don't understand now, but afterward you will know." This was too much for Peter. He exclaimed, "You will never wash my feet—ever!"

Peter was appalled. Jesus, his Lord and Savior, the Messiah, the most important person in the room, in his life, and the universe was attempting to wash his feet. This was work for servants, lowly servants who were supposed to do dirty work. Not Jesus! Peter once again found himself telling the Lord what he could and could not do. And once again, Jesus had to remind Peter what the title "Lord" means. Jesus determines his course of action without consulting anyone else or obtaining anyone's permission.

"If I don't wash you, you have no part with Me," Jesus rebuked Peter. The threat of exclusion stung. Peter replied, "Lord, not only my feet, but also my hands and my head." This is one of the more humorous statements in Scripture. The subject matter, receiving service from Jesus authenticating belief in him, is certainly a serious matter. The imagery is comical, however, as Peter asks for a whole bath. Jesus' reply returns the focus to the key issue—his example of service by foot-washing—while borrowing Peter's bathing analogy to make the cogent point that one disciple's faith was illegitimate.

Jesus finished washing their feet and resumed his place at the table to teach the disciples why he had done it. He said, "You call Me Teacher and Lord. This is well said, for I am. So if I, your Lord and Teacher, have washed your feet, you also ought to wash one another's feet. For I have given you an example that you also should do just as I have done for you."

While some have interpreted this literally—meaning foot-washing is a required church practice—most understand Jesus' actions as an object lesson to teach the importance of maintaining a servant's spirit in leadership. Jesus used this incident to powerfully communicate this principle: the essence of Christian leadership is service.

Christian leadership is often equated with servant leadership. What does this mean? Are Christian leaders only leading when they are doing menial or practical things for their followers? Is it possible to be a servant leader when your breadth of responsibility makes personal ministry to hundreds or thousands of followers impossible? Younger leaders are often zealous and ambitious. Are these qualities compatible with Christian leadership?

Servanthood in leadership is both an action and an attitude. Let's consider each category and discover how they apply to Christian leaders. Servant actions are important for every leader. A servant attitude in all our actions is equally important.

Servant leadership involves practical acts of service to meet the needs of others. No matter how large your leadership responsibility, you will always have some people who work closely with you. Every leader, including those in executive or senior leadership roles, can still meet the practical needs of those who work most closely with them. Jesus modeled this when he washed the feet of the Twelve.

A more difficult question: "How do you serve a large number of people in a growing church or expanding ministry organization?" The answer is also exemplified by Jesus who "did not consider equality with God as something to be used for His own advantage. Instead He emptied Himself by assuming the form of a slave. . . . He humbled Himself by becoming obedient to the point of death—even to death on a cross" (Phil. 2:6–8). Jesus had "equality with God" but "emptied himself" to make redemption possible for all humankind. Jesus models this leadership principle: use your leadership position for the benefit of your followers. Servant leadership doesn't deny the influence, power, and authority that rests in your leadership role, but it does use those resources for the benefit of your followers, not to feather your own nest or further your own career.

Acts of service aren't necessarily defined by how menial they are—even though the foot-washing illustration might point to that conclusion. Service is defined more by its outcome—the benefit of others—than by the essence of the work performed. For example, preaching can be a self-aggrandizing show or it can be a self-sacrificing offering. Motive and results determine the difference. Giving money can also go either way—self-promotion or selfless sacrifice. When you give to benefit others and not for what you will get out of it (monetarily or emotionally), your giving demonstrates servant leadership. Christian leaders focus their acts of service on meeting the needs of their followers, not on making themselves look good. Servant leadership is an attitude. Most leaders, as their responsibility grows, do fewer and fewer personal acts to support their followers or facilitate their ministry's mission.

How can you develop a servant spirit, particularly when your scope of responsibility broadens and you are no longer expected to do the so-called dirty work?

First, choose to do a dirty job. Don was rapidly progressing in executive leadership in a secular company. He became convicted about increasing pride. He told his pastor, "The next time you have a dirty job at the church, call me." A few days later, a major sewage backup had several toilets erupting at once. The pastor called Don and said, "I think we have that dirty job you were looking for." Don arrived within minutes, told everyone to leave for the day, and spent the evening cleaning the church. He later told us it really changed his attitude for the better. Choosing to do a dirty job will refocus you on serving others.

As a seminary president, I don't mow the lawn, paint walls, or make copies for professors. The seminary depends on me to serve by doing other things—assignments only the president can accomplish given my experience, resources, and relationships. This doesn't mean, however, I am too good to do those hands-on tasks. While there are some tasks I don't do—for the good of the seminary—there are no tasks I am too good to do. When leaders puff up with self-importance saying, "There are just certain things I won't do," their servant spirits have vanished. Their attitude is wrong, no matter their actions, and it will ultimately undermine their leadership effectiveness.

Second, choose to serve anonymously. The more notoriety you have as a leader, the harder it is to do this. Our ministry decided to build a large facility with volunteer labor. Every holiday weekend, teams would come to work. I worked with them, not telling them I was the organization's chief executive. Giving my holiday time and working manually just like the other men helped me to refocus. God uses secret service to revive a servant spirit.

Third, choose to serve a critic. Not everyone will like you. Leaders often manage difficult relationships. Serving those who criticize you is a means God uses to purify leadership motives. One of my critics once came to me with a life crisis—his son had impregnated another church leader's daughter. He asked for my help . . . not long after he had publicly attacked my integrity. I was tempted to turn him away but chose instead to help him as best I could. Through the process, two good things happened: my leadership motives were tested and purified, and a new friendship was formed.

Jesus modeled servant leadership when he washed the disciples' feet. While you may not literally wash feet, you aren't too good to do it if that's your assignment from Jesus. More important, you must approach every task with a servant spirit. Set aside your own interests and use your leadership position and influence for the good of others.

QUESTIONS FOR REFLECTION

1. Are you tempted to use your leadership position for self-serving gain? How do you resist this temptation?
2. Are there any jobs that you are too important to do? Why or why not?
3. What is your plan for sharpening your servant-leader attitude?

Lesson 17

BEWARE OF BRAVADO

Matthew 26:31–35; Mark 14:27–31;
Luke 22:31–34; John 13:36–38

 One of the Bible's authenticating features is the honest way it describes the failures and shortcomings of prominent characters. We see biblical characters—warts and all—as they struggled to learn what it meant to follow Jesus and fulfill the leadership roles he assigned. On the heels of the remarkable foot-washing story, Peter made one of those blunders which reveals much about his character and the struggle he faced in following Jesus. This story is so important that all four Gospel writers included it. God must really want us to learn its lesson.

As Jesus drew closer to the cross, his instructions to the disciples became more pointed and poignant. He told them he would soon be going away, and they couldn't go with him. He challenged them to love one another after he was gone—both by modeling his love to others and by underscoring their need to support one another during trials to come. Jesus foreshadowed his violent death and the persecution that would follow. As these dire predictions mounted, Peter's frustration also increased. His response to Jesus was an emotional eruption promising far more than he could and would deliver.

Peter promised Jesus, "I'm ready to go with You both to prison and to death."

"Even if everyone runs away because of You, I will never run away!" He continued, insisting, "I will lay down my life for You!" Those were bold but ultimately empty words from an emerging leader who meant well. His intent, while admirable, was more bravado than bravery. In the emotion of the moment, he rashly promised far more than he was spiritually prepared to deliver.

An old rancher once described a person to me as "all hat, no cattle." The same man—a font of colorful clichés—also warned me, "Never let your mouth write a check your fists can't cash." Translation: don't make bold statements you can't back up. Peter's statements fall into this category. He meant well, but he promised far more than he was able to deliver. Beyond that, his statements smack of the arrogant belief that he was somehow immune to the potential failures to which all of us are susceptible.

Several years ago, several prominent media ministers who had succumbed to immorality were exposed over a few weeks' time. They were disgraced, their ministries came unraveled, and all the good they had accomplished was called into question. All ministry leaders were affected as their integrity was called into question, damaged by the failures of those more well-known. As a younger leader trying to establish my own reputation, their failures angered me. It was hard enough to overcome my own mistakes and earn ministerial trust without having to overcome the sins of others.

Gary, a good friend and former Marine, stopped by my office. We were talking about various church issues when the media ministry failures were mentioned. With an appropriate amount of puffed-up, righteous indignation, I said, "Well, those guys are disgusting. They have embarrassed themselves and hurt all of us in ministry leadership. One thing's for sure—nothing like that will ever happen to me."

Gary just glared at me, eyes wide and nostrils flared. His Marine stare was intimidating. He looked like a drill sergeant about to explode, but when he spoke it was barely above a whisper. He said, "What you just said is the most dangerous thing I've ever heard come out of your mouth. It *can* happen to you. If you don't change your attitude, it *will* happen to you. If you think you're immune to moral failure, you're ripe for it to happen.

Get your guard up. Stop thinking it can't happen to you and make sure it doesn't."

That confrontation with Gary has stayed with me for thirty years. He was right on every count. My comments revealed the arrogance of my false belief that moral temptation was something I had mastered. My words definitely wrote a check the rest of me couldn't cash. Gary had the courage to call me on it. His warning that I was most vulnerable when I claimed invulnerability was dead right. His challenge to get my guard up—and keep it up—was just what I needed to hear.

Jesus confronted Peter in a similar way. When Peter promised perpetual loyalty, Jesus confronted him with reality. Jesus told Peter he would deny him three times before the morning rooster crowed. Peter was startled but refused to believe it. He replied, "Even if I have to die with You, I will never deny You. I will lay down my life for You!" Peter's leadership influence is seen in how the other disciples responded. A chorus of support ensued with everyone promising to stand with Jesus—even to the point of death. As we know in hindsight, those well-intended promises were without substance. Within hours, the disciple were scattered, and Peter had profanely denied any relationship with Jesus. His bravado, expressed in rash promises, revealed his pride and masked his fear. He may have meant well and actually believed what he was saying, but his promises could not and did not withstand the crucible of subsequent events.

Emerging leaders must learn to measure their words, avoid bravado, and speak truthfully about their commitments, expertise, and convictions. It's so tempting to talk big—to overstate issues to appear stronger, wiser, and more devoted than you really are. Doing this creates unrealistic expectations, but more dangerously, it also inflates false confidence. You will begin to read your own press clippings, thinking more highly of yourself than you should and underscoring a phony sense of well-being.

One common example of ministerial bravado is to boldly claim what you would do if you were leading in a given situation. You loudly announce what you would do if that happened in your church, your home, or your community, etc. Frankly, you don't know what you would do. You only know what you hope you would do, but without the distorting impact of emotional attachment to a situation, it's impossible to predict what you would actually do. Your presumptuous statements communicate insensitivity and emotional detachment. Your followers won't gain confidence in you because of your supposed certainty. They will more likely distance themselves from you, being turned off by your lack of emotional intelligence and failure to acknowledge the complexity of the circumstances. Beware of claiming ultimate insight into complicated situations you observe only from a distance.

Leaders also sometimes pontificate on doctrinal positions or biblical interpretations as if their understanding of those issues is the final word. One younger leader e-mailed me and asked me to help get him on the program at a national religious convention. He wrote, "I can clear up all the tensions surrounding Calvinism in twenty minutes with some insights God has given me on the subject." That would be a very powerful twenty minutes—reconciling the combined intellectual output of the church for the past four hundred years! Holding convictions about doctrinal and biblical position is part of ministry leadership. Doing so with respect for others who disagree is a mark of wisdom, not weakness. Beware of claiming you have the final word on every subject.

A final example of ministerial bravado is claiming more than is true about your personal spiritual practices. Ministry leaders feel pressured—and rightly so—to be examples in areas like prayer, witnessing, and giving. There's a subtle temptation to inflate our actual experience in order to inspire our followers. The opposite approach is more effective. Strive to be an example in these areas and others, all the while being honest with your followers about your progress. People know their leaders aren't perfect and become suspicious when they claim to be. It's better to acknowledge the struggles as well as the victories on the way toward spiritual maturity. Doing so inspires your followers far more than a false model of supposed perfection. Beware of inflating your spirituality to impress others.

Peter made bold claims that he didn't back up with his actions. Bravado is tempting, but ultimately it will be embarrassing and humbling when you finally have to acknowledge the truth. Be wise with your words. Say what you mean, mean what you say, and say no more. Your humility and honesty will inspire your followers far more than bold, empty words.

QUESTIONS FOR REFLECTION

1. Have you made any promises to God or others that you regret? What do you need to do to make things right?
2. Do you believe you are above failing or above being questioned in certain areas?
3. To which of the three examples of ministerial bravado are you most susceptible? What is your plan to prevent future failure in that area?

Lesson 18

STAY ALERT

Matthew 26:36–46; Mark 14:32–42; Luke 22:39–46

 Training to be a leader is wearisome. The disciples had had a full day with Jesus, culminating in what would turn out to be their final meal together. They had learned important lessons that day about serving humbly and avoiding bravado. They had learned that Jesus' death was imminent and were puzzled about what was about to unfold. It had been a long, emotionally exhausting, and spiritually depleting day. They were ready for bed, but Jesus had other plans and other needs.

Jesus took the disciples to a garden in Gethsemane to pray. He left the larger group behind, taking Peter, James, and John with him a little farther. Jesus told them about the anguish he was feeling. He then asked them to wait while he slipped away to pray alone. The nearness of his death was closing in on him as he cried out, "My Father! If it is possible, let this cup pass from Me. Yet not as I will, but as You will." Jesus then returned to Peter and found him and the others sleeping (along with the others). He asked, "Couldn't you stay awake with Me one hour? Stay awake and pray, so that you won't enter into temptation. The spirit is willing, but the flesh is weak."

Jesus left again for private prayer. He returned to find Peter and the others asleep again. He left them alone and went back to his prayer place. Finally, he returned the third time and found them still sleeping. By that time, there was no need to awaken them. His betrayers had arrived, and Jesus would soon be arrested. The passion events were now underway, moving inexorably to their inevitable, horrific end.

The repeated trips that Jesus made back to the sleeping disciples are interesting details in the story. Jesus, facing death on the cross, longed for human companionship at his darkest hour. His communion with God was powerful—Son to Father in the purest form. Yet, it apparently didn't fully satisfy his relational or spiritual needs. Jesus wanted his closest followers, his most trusted companions, with him as he prepared for the cross. His pathos-filled pleas to pray with him for even one hour reveal his desire for spiritual support and brotherly fellowship. The physical fatigue, relational insensitivity, and spiritual dullness of the disciples—even the inner circle of Peter, James, and John—all contributed to their sleeping through the darkest night of Jesus' life. When he needed friends the most, they failed him on every count. When Jesus needed his companions to be most spiritually alert, they were asleep.

Jesus' threefold return to find Peter sleeping foreshadows and parallels Peter's threefold denial of Jesus the following day. When Peter denied Jesus and heard the rooster crow, perhaps he thought of Jesus rousing him three times the previous night. Jesus needed Peter three times in the night and was neglected. He needed Peter three times the next day and was denied. How painful this must have been as Peter remembered these threesomes later in his life.

Peter failed Jesus at a crucial time for three reasons: physical fatigue, relational insensitivity, and spiritual dullness. Leaders must stay alert and responsive to God at work in and around us. Emerging leaders must discipline themselves so they are at their best when leadership demands are the strongest.

When legitimate leadership demands tire you out, there's not much you can do about it. But when fatigue is caused by failure to manage your schedule, exercise enough, or eat properly, you can't blame your leadership role. When you are tired, you will make poor decisions and lose your spiritual edge. One pastor was dismissed for falsifying his expense account. When asked why he did it, he said, "The church has taken so much out of me, I thought they owed me the money." He told me of working week after week without a vacation or a single day off—so he lied about ministry trips and pocketed the money. His reason was a cop-out. The church hadn't taken so much out of him. He was addicted to being needed, so he developed workaholic patterns to salve his insecurity. Over time, his fatigue—not daily fatigue, but being bone-tired from prolonged overextension—clouded his judgment. He was no longer alert to God's Spirit convicting him of poor decisions or sensitive to God's wisdom guiding his choices. Fatigue from a mismanaged schedule, rooted in unresolved insecurities, destroyed his credibility.

You can also miss opportunities for ministry through relational insensitivity. Some leaders, me included, lack spontaneous sensitivity to people on a deeply emotional level. For many years, I blamed other people for my deficiency and excused my callousness. If I had been in the garden with Jesus, I would have been sleeping just like Peter. I would have been oblivious to Jesus' need for companionship and his intense spiritual battle. If you struggle like this, how can you increase your sensitivity to the needs of people? Paying attention to four major life transitions and knowing that every person is emotionally vulnerable when they happen has revolutionized my capacity for interpersonal ministry. The four transitions are: people die, relationships struggle, health fails, and things break.

While these four categories aren't all-inclusive, they cover a vast number of situations requiring relational connectivity. When anyone in my relational circle goes through any of these circumstances, it behooves me to connect with them more intentionally. Events connected to the death of a loved one seem like obvious times when people need personal ministry. It's embarrassing to admit, but I didn't fully understand that as a younger leader. Fortunately, the deacons in my first pastorate were in tune with bereavement ministry and taught me how important it was. Be alert to grieving people. God is at work, and they need you in those moments.

Relational struggles range from the obvious, like a divorce, to the less significant (unless you are the person involved), like a teenage romance gone bad. Broken engagements, sibling disputes over an inheritance, and families dealing with military deployments are examples of when people need relational support. Anytime a person experiences disruption in their most meaningful relationships (as they define them, not as you think they should be defined), they are open to receiving ministry. Be alert to people experiencing relational tension or change. God is at work and they need your guidance.

As a young leader, my insensitivity to sick people was not as bad as my ignorance about grief, but it was close. Through my own bout with cancer, the importance of ministering to the sick and being cared for while ailing became very personal. On the morning of my first cancer surgery, three older couples from our church were waiting at the hospital when we arrived before dawn. "What are you doing here?" I asked. Their reply burned into my soul and brings tears to my eyes as I type it now. "We're standing by," they said. Jesus asked Peter to do the same thing in his darkest hour—just to be there for him. I was facing my worst life circumstance, and rather than sleep through the night, these couples rose up early and came to stand by with my wife and children. They stood with me, too, as I could feel their presence, just knowing they were close. Be alert for people grappling with illness. God is at work, and they need your support.

When things break—using the broadest definition of "things"—people are similarly vulnerable. These circumstances might include a car accident, home burglary, house fire, investment loss, foreclosure, or bankruptcy. Despite our attempts to distance ourselves from these entanglements, Christians still struggle when their things—often an extension or personification of their identity—are damaged. Rather than criticize their warped priorities, first step in with compassionate ministry. God will convict of misplaced affections in his own time. Leave that to him. Be alert for people struggling with broken things. God is at work, and they need your understanding.

Jesus was dealing with some of these challenges at Gethsemane. He was facing death, he was in relational crisis with God and the disciples, and he was about to suffer physically. He needed private prayer as well as the fellowship and spiritual support of his friends. Peter and the other disciples failed him. Jesus reproved them to be alert to his needs and the coming spiritual battle.

Emerging leaders must learn the discipline of spiritual and relational alertness. You must learn to recognize God's activity by considering likely circumstances indicating a person is experiencing God's work. Get your spiritual antennae up. Pay attention to the indicators that people are experiencing life's challenges and searching for spiritual help and personal support. Step in boldly with ministry to meet needs and deepen faith. Be alert and take action—don't sleep through moments pregnant with opportunity for ministry.

QUESTIONS FOR REFLECTION

1. What blunts your spiritual senses most—physical fatigue, relational insensitivity, or spiritual dullness? What will you do about this?
2. What additional indicators besides the four listed above can alert you to people who are in need of and open to ministry?
3. What can you do to hone your spiritual alertness to the needs of others?

RESTRAIN YOURSELF

Matthew 26:47–56; Mark 14:43–50;
Luke 22:47–53; John 18:1–11

Jesus' all-night prayer meeting culminated with a mob arresting Jesus and taking him into custody. Peter was outraged and panicky. He drew his sword and slashed at the crowd, cutting off the right ear of Malchus, the high priest's servant. Typical Peter—impetuous action trying to solve the wrong problem the wrong way at the wrong time and in the wrong place. He was tired (having slept fitfully the previous night), probably hungry (the mob arrived near daybreak), and intimidated by what was happening. Jesus' recent predictions of his death and Peter's denials may have been reverberating through Peter's mind. It was time to put a stop to all this—off with their heads!

Jesus rebuked Peter strongly, restored Malchus' ear, and condemned the violence. He told Peter to put away his sword lest he die by the same means. Jesus then asked three rhetorical questions: "Do you think that I cannot call on My Father, and He will provide Me at once with more than 12 legions of angels?" and "How, then, would the Scriptures be fulfilled that say it must happen this way?" and "Am I not to drink the cup the Father has given Me?" Jesus reminded the mob he had taught openly in the temple many times and was never arrested, but his capture had to unfold in such a way as to fulfill the prophecies about him. Peter, accompanied by the remaining eleven disciples, then made his second rash, spur-of-the-moment decision of the night. He deserted Jesus.

Impetuosity is a common quality of younger leaders. Many haven't yet learned the discipline of self-restraint. It's difficult to wait for God's timing to be revealed when it seems he's being slow to act. Peter thought Jesus' situation was desperate. Jesus had a different perspective. He understood God's plan, timing, and purpose in the events. Peter's limited perspective, physical fatigue, spiritual dullness, and impulsive personality all contributed to his choice to whip out his sword and start fighting. No matter the reason, when a leader acts impulsively, the result is almost always bad.

While Peter's dilemma in Gethsemane was unique, the principle of practicing self-restraint in the face of troubling circumstances when God seems slow to act applies in many leadership situations. Self-control is a fruit of the Holy Spirit. Practicing self-restraint requires spiritual motivation and wise personal choices, often under pressure. It's hard to hold back when everything within you wants to lash out or move forward. Taking charge of your emotions and measuring your response in heated moments is an essential leadership skill. This principle applies in several areas.

Emerging leaders must learn self-restraint in how they express themselves. While it may seem cathartic to give someone a piece of your mind in the moment, the collateral damage will diminish your satisfaction. Back in the day, this usually involved being careful with what you said or what you wrote in a letter. These days, the problem is exacerbated by e-mail, text messaging, and social media. It's tempting to reply to a hostile e-mail or Facebook post with brashness beyond what you would say face-to-face. This kind of communication is almost never productive.

A few years ago, a person wrote a presumptive e-mail critical of my leadership. His message was based on misinformation, outright lies, and conclusions from his own delusional thinking. It made me mad. I wrote him back, in very plain terms, correcting the record and confronting his pompous attitude. He then replied with, "Thank you. I will now post both my e-mail and your reply on my website." *Gotcha!* Like an animal lured into a trap, I had fallen for the gambit and responded in a way he could use to further attack me. It would have been better to practice self-restraint with this irrational critic. A limited response or no response at all would have been more appropriate—less satisfying in the moment, but also less damaging over the long haul.

Emerging leaders must also learn self-restraint in decision-making. It's tempting to plow ahead, even when God puts stop or yield signs in our way to redirect us. A major area where self-restraint seems lacking today is borrowing money to build ministry facilities. Rather than waiting on God's provision, the prevailing counsel is to borrow, build, and hope the people attracted by the buildings pay them off. That's a good strategy unless something unexpected happens. One church had a moral failure by a staff pastor just after borrowing several million dollars. Dozens of families left immediately. Today, that church is closed—after defaulting on its bonds and defrauding hundreds of Christian investors. Debt advocates seldom consider the full ramifications of their decisions—the "what ifs" of economic downturn or leadership failure. While borrowing may have its place in some situations, doing so because you've lost patience waiting for God to provide through other means is never wise.

Self-restraint must also be evident in other areas like supervising an assistant, managing your expense account, or maintaining boundaries in your work environment. Leaders have privileges and can easily manipulate circumstances to their advantage. Making self-limiting choices is difficult. After all, rank supposedly has its privileges. Wise leaders know that rank has more responsibility than it has privileges.

Learning self-restraint begins by recognizing that self-control is a Holy Spirit-produced character quality. Entitlement isn't a fruit of the Spirit or the special purview of leaders. The opposite is actually true. You must model self-control in the face of peer pressure tempting you otherwise, as you demonstrate consistent discipline as a Spirit-controlled leader. When you do this, your followers will appreciate your spiritual maturity and the decision-making discipline that results.

Another step toward self-restraint is learning to talk less and speak more carefully. Leaders seldom have to apologize for or clean up damage from what they did not say. It's especially important to measure your words when you are tired, angry, or frustrated. Every parent knows children are more prone to behaving badly in those conditions. Like everyone else, leaders are human, and are also susceptible to poor choices when life has worn them down. Be careful what you say when you are agitated or vulnerable.

Harsh words vent emotions, but they seldom produce lasting leadership results. You may intimidate someone into immediate action, but you won't motivate them to sustained excellence. You may win an argument but lose a follower. You may answer a critic but also inflame more vitriolic attacks. Many leaders are gifted speakers, able to use words in influential ways. Those same gifts, when used negatively, inflict damage very difficult to overcome. Controlling your words is one way to model self-restraint.

Controlling your emotions, particularly in decision-making, is a third area of self-restraint leaders must learn. The two most troublesome emotions for leaders are fear and anger. Fear makes you timid—afraid to do the right thing, the right way, at the right time. Making decisions or not making decisions based on fear leads to shortsighted, least-common-denominator results rather than bold, innovative, visionary actions. Angry decisions have the same result, only from different motives. Anger prompts rash decisions which may produce immediate relief but without long-range profitability. When a leader responds in anger, the result usually damages relationship—the hard currency of Christian leadership. This is never positive for the individuals involved or the organization impacted.

Self-restraint with your emotions doesn't mean you deny them or ignore them. It means you own your emotions. You admit that you are afraid or angry—owning the emotion—but you do not allow it to control you. Like an old-time cowboy, you brand the emotion for what it is and then pen it up until you get the decision made. While emotions buck and jump, trying to get your attention, decisions are made outside the corral. Self-restraint acknowledges the emotional currency at play in any decision, but decides every matter based on the organization's mission, vision, and values. Leaders must make mission-disciplined decisions, not those driven by fear or anger.

Self-restraint in the face of challenging circumstances is your leadership responsibility. Put the sword away and do what's right—not what feels good in the moment.

QUESTIONS FOR REFLECTION

1. Give an example of a rash decision you made that you regret. How did you manage the damage?

2. Do you struggle with controlling communication? What will you do to improve in this area?

3. Are you prone to decision-making dominated by fear or anger? Why? What will you do about this problem?

Lesson 20

FAILURE HAPPENS

Matthew 26:57–75; Mark 14:53–72;
Luke 22:54–62; John 18:15–27

Peter's worst moments happened while Jesus was on trial for his life. He had trailed behind the arresting crowd to see what would happen to Jesus. We should give Peter at least some credit. While most of the disciples ran away when Jesus was arrested, he at least came back to see the events unfold firsthand. While Peter was waiting in the courtyard, a slave girl asked him if he was one of Jesus' followers. He denied it. A little while later, some of the bystanders asked if he were a disciple. Once again, he denied knowing Jesus. Finally, a slave of the high priest and a relative of Malchus, the man who had lost his ear, asked Peter if he had been with Jesus in Gethsemane. Peter denied being with Jesus, cursing and swearing his disavowal.

A rooster crowed. That may have been the saddest sound ever heard in human history. That threefold denial Jesus had warned about and Peter had vehemently denied even possible, had happened. Peter fled the court-yard, weeping bitterly at his disloyalty to Jesus. His Lord and Savior had been arrested, was facing death, and he, Peter, had abandoned him entirely. He had failed miserably and completely.

After three years with Jesus, Peter certainly had expected more of himself. All the time they had spent together, all the lessons learned, and all the good times they had shared should have mattered for something. Peter was personally trained by Jesus to be the leader after he left. He had failed completely in his first big test as the person in charge when Jesus was removed from leading the disciples. Peter failed on several levels.

First, Peter had failed as a friend. Jesus had invited him into his inner relational circle and had given him unusual access over the previous three years. Think of all they had been through together—good and bad. From healings to feedings to near riots, Peter had been right beside Jesus. Can you also imagine the hundreds of additional days they spent together not described in the Gospels? Their personal relationship was profound. While we sing, "What a friend we have in Jesus," Peter really knew him personally and intimately.

Second, Peter failed the other disciples. Over the years, Jesus had trained him to lead the others. Peter was continually singled out for special attention from Jesus. He is often portrayed with James and John, the inner circle around Jesus receiving extra training. Along with that privilege came added responsibility—leading the Twelve. Peter's actions at Gethsemane—sleeping through the prayer meeting and pulling his sword to defend Jesus—were leadership failures. When Jesus was arrested, everyone ran away—including Peter. When the group needed a leader to hold them together and give them perspective, Peter failed them all.

Peter also failed himself, denying who he was and his role in God's kingdom. He rejected his identity, lied about his whereabouts, and refused to admit who he was or how he was related to Jesus. His loathsome, profane denial of all he had lived over the previous three years was a complete rejection of the man he had become. While running away was cowardly, denying his identity was even worse.

Ultimately, Peter also failed God. Jesus was God, and Jesus prayed to God the night before his arrest. Peter didn't participate in the prayer meeting. He also didn't remember or recognize Jesus' authority in the critical moment of his arrest. He panicked, thinking Jesus was powerless to do anything about what was happening to him. Peter seized the moment, assuming his self-effort would somehow win the day.

Peter failed. Even after years of close friendship with Jesus, in-depth personal training, perfect modeling of ministry leadership, and learning about his future kingdom role, Peter failed. As a younger leader, you may find this troubling, even depressing. Peter was personally selected and trained by Jesus, yet he still failed miserably at a crucial moment. As an emerging leader, you are probably very aware of your weaknesses. Your propensity to make mistakes, even when you are trying to do your best, is frustrating. You are persistent in your efforts to improve, but your two clay feet keep tripping you up. No matter how hard you try, you still fail in crucial ways and at inopportune moments.

You hope this will get better over time. You hope your character development will eliminate some besetting sins. You hope your improving leadership skills will prevent mistakes. You really hope your worst problems—like being controlled by fear or anger—will abate through prayer and personal growth. Good news: Most of these issues get better with focused effort, intense training, and by learning from experience. But there is also bad news: No matter how hard you try, you will continue to make leadership mistakes. No matter how much you grow, your character flaws will still occasionally embarrass you and undermine your most significant relationships and accomplishments.

On the twenty-fifth anniversary of my ministry leadership, I reflected on what I had learned about myself as a leader. After thinking and praying about it for a while, I set aside some time to write my insights. Here is my first sentence: "After twenty-five years, I thought I would be a better man." There was no second sentence. My overwhelming conclusion after years of ministry leadership is that any good that has happened has been in spite of me, not because of me. My sins and shortcomings haven't gone away. They are lessened in some ways, but in other ways, they are more sophisticated and deceitful. Fake holiness and trumped up confidence may temporarily mask some of my weaknesses, but they always bloom out in the end.

It's been ten years since I wrote that sentence, and my status hasn't changed. I really thought I would be less angry, more insightful, less stressed, and more prayerful by now. I thought I would be a model of wisdom, a font of knowledge, and an example of courage under fire. I thought I would have all the answers—or at least most of them—to thorny problems and prickly people. Instead, I find myself guessing at solutions and avoiding dealing with difficult people. I thought I would be more honest, but I still find myself scheming to make myself look good and faking it so people won't criticize me. In short, failure—personally and professionally—is still very much a part of who I am. I'm better in some areas, but still woefully inadequate in others. I've learned leadership skills but not nearly enough to be confident when facing the most challenging issues. My character is more refined, but the more I become like Jesus in some areas, the more I'm aware of my shortcomings in others.

As a younger leader, you may read this and be discouraged, but please consider another conclusion. You are frail and will fail. Your shortcomings are more than quirks and colorful qualities. They are character flaws that you will battle your entire life. You will never be perfect—but God will use you anyway. The story of Peter's failure is, ultimately, a story of God's grace. God chooses and uses us as we are—not as we think we should be—to accomplish his work. God has largely limited himself to working through people today—and that's a huge limitation. Just think—the same God who spoke a universe into existence now depends on you to speak his message. Without your preaching, teaching, and witnessing, the gospel won't be shared. God chooses and uses people like you, weaknesses and all, to get his work done.

Peter's failure shouldn't serve as an indictment to discourage you from becoming a leader. It's an encouragement that God, even with your weaknesses, can accomplish his work through you. That's very good news! You are flawed, yes. But God will still use you to lead others to advance his kingdom. While you are responsible to learn all you can and grow to be like Jesus in every way possible, your usefulness is more dependent on God's grace than your effort. He has called you to leadership—so lead. You will fail. You will disappoint yourself, your followers, and God—but lead anyway. As we will see in the following sections of this book, Peter's failures didn't disqualify him from significant leadership in the early church and from leaving a legacy for the church for all time. Flawed people can still make a profound leadership contribution.

QUESTIONS FOR REFLECTION

1. What sins or shortcomings do you use as excuses to disqualify you from consideration as a leader? Why is this wrong?
2. What is your worst leadership failure so far? How have you overcome it to continue to fulfill your leadership responsibilities?
3. What is the most encouraging part of your past leadership failures?

RESTORATION IS POSSIBLE

John 21:1–23

After Jesus' death and Peter's abandonment (Peter is conspicuously absent from the Gospel's record of the people who accompanied Jesus to the cross or cared for his body after the crucifixion), the disciples were disconcerted and confused. One evening, seven of them were together when Peter announced, "I'm going fishing." Some commentators see this as a further rejection of his call to leave fishing and follow Jesus, but it may have been less insidious. Perhaps the disciples were simply hungry. Maybe they needed some quick cash to meet immediate needs. Could it be they just wanted to return to something familiar while they sorted out what to do next?

The night fishing trip was futile. They caught nothing. On the way to shore, a man called out, "You don't have any fish, do you?" Then he told them to cast their nets on the right side of their boat. They immediately caught so many fish they couldn't haul them onboard. John realized who was on the shore and called out, "It is the Lord!"

When Peter heard that, he grabbed his outer garment and jumped into the sea. He swam one hundred yards to shore, anxious to get to Jesus as soon as possible. The disciples followed in the boat, bringing what turned out to be a huge catch of 153 fish with them. When the whole group got on shore, they discovered Jesus had already built a fire, was roasting some fish, and had bread ready to eat. He invited the group to share breakfast with him. What a joyous time it was—but what might Peter have felt, given his memories of the last time he saw Jesus?

The fire Jesus had built on the beach is specifically called a "charcoal fire." This is only the second time this description of a fire is used in the Gospels. The other instance described the fire Peter warmed himself by in the courtyard when he denied Jesus. The smell of the charcoal may have kindled painful memories for Peter and set the stage for what was about to happen.

When breakfast was over, Jesus brought up the issue of Peter's abandonment in a pointed way. He asked Peter, "Do you love Me more than these?" Who or what were the "these" in Jesus' question? Some postulate the disciples; some the fishing business. Both may have been included in Jesus' generalization. Whatever Jesus meant, Peter got the point. He replied, "Yes, Lord, You know that I love You." Jesus told Peter to, "Feed My lambs." Then Jesus asked the same question again. Peter answered accordingly and Jesus told him to "Shepherd My sheep." Then Jesus asked the same question a third time.

Jesus had been building to this third question from the beginning. He was confronting Peter subtly by evoking the memory of his threefold denial just days before. Jesus drew Peter's guilt and shame to the surface with pointed questions that cut to the core of his being. We're told that Peter was grieved when Jesus asked the question the third time. He responded, "Lord, You know everything! You know that I love you." The plaintive tone of the response reveals Peter's earnest, pleading desire to reestablish his relationship with Jesus. Yes, Jesus knew everything. Jesus knew what he was saying, and the confrontation was both symbolic and surgical. The context was a reminder of a past fishing experience when Jesus called Peter, the charcoal fire brought attention to his duplicity in the courtyard, and the threefold questions underscored Peter's threefold denial. The building intensity in the conversation also paralleled Peter's progressive intensity in denying Jesus, ending with profanity and cursing to underscore his position.

Jesus gave a much longer response to Peter's third answer. He again told Peter, "Feed My sheep," but then he added a very significant prediction about the future. Jesus told Peter he would die by crucifixion. He contrasted Peter's youthful freedom with the all-encompassing burden he would bear as a Christian leader in the future. His love for Jesus was genuine, but it would be tested to the max. He would face martyrdom in a similar fashion as Jesus had given his life. Jesus then said, "Follow Me!"

Peter may have been stunned by what he heard. He pointed to John standing nearby and asked Jesus, "What about him?" Did this question reveal curious concern for another inner circle member or was it another attempt by Peter to deflect attention from his responsibilities? Jesus' answer doesn't reveal which it was, only that what happened to or for others shouldn't be his concern. Jesus essentially said, "That's my business," and then he gave Peter his final instruction—"Follow Me."

We have already established the totality of Peter's failure—both in his relationship to Jesus and leadership of the disciples. This conversation records the rest of the story. Peter was fully restored to his status as a disciple and leader through a painful process which involved confronting his failures. Jesus didn't ignore what Peter had done. He confronted him skillfully and thoroughly, allowing him to grieve over his actions and take responsibility for them. When it was over, Jesus' final words reveal the fullness of the restoration.

Peter was recommissioned as both a follower and a leader. He was reinstated fully and given meaningful work to do—feed, shepherd, and care for Jesus' people. Jesus said, "Follow Me," and expected Peter to fulfill that directive. The confidence Jesus had in Peter's future faithfulness is also subtly but powerfully included in this story. Jesus prophesied that Peter would die a martyr's death by crucifixion. This implies three things. First, Peter would remain faithful from this point forward in his life. Second, Peter would remain steadfast through a death involving prolonged suffering. Finally, Peter would die as a martyr—faithful to the end and an example of self-sacrificing commitment. Jesus' prophecy confirms Peter's restoration as a leader and predicts his future faithfulness in that role. Peter was fully restored.

You will make leadership mistakes. You will fail both personally and professionally in fulfilling your leadership role. You will also sin—sometimes in very destructive ways. You may make lousy personnel choices, waste money on pointless projects, and chase ego-driven pipe dreams. You will blow it so badly some days that you will be sure your church or ministry should fire you and God should put you on the shelf. When you think all is lost, Jesus will surprise you. He will restore you as his follower and put you back into leadership.

When—not if, but when—you fail in the future, here's the recipe for restoration. First, admit your mistake. Tell God about it. Tell your board or church leaders. Tell the people who were negatively impacted by your decision. Everyone—and I mean everyone—already knows you aren't perfect. Admitting it won't be news. Some leaders are reluctant to admit their mistakes; they wrongly assume that acknowledging mistakes diminishes leadership stature. The opposite is true. Followers admire leaders who tell the truth, even about their mistakes.

Second, if it was more than a mistake—if it involved sin—confess it to God and whoever was involved in the situation. Not all leadership mistakes are sinful, but some are. Be sure you confess your sin appropriately and receive the forgiveness God and others offer.

Third, accept the consequences of your actions. Many leaders fail the restoration process at this crucial point. Admitting mistakes and confessing sin doesn't lessen the consequences of your actions. You may lose some privileges, be asked to make restitution, or otherwise clean up what you have done. This part of restoration is often rejected by leaders who feel things should be forgiven and forgotten. Don't make this mistake. Humble yourself by accepting your consequences. Restoration is usually a process. It starts at a specific point in time but progresses over a few weeks or months. Allow time for people time to heal and for emotional trust to be rebuilt.

Finally, move on. Once a mistake is admitted or sin is confessed and forgiven and consequences are fulfilled or mitigated, the issue is over. Let it die. Bury it and stop digging it up to check its lack of pulse. There's nothing gained from reliving your past mistakes or continually reminding others of theirs. This only leads to condemnation—the perpetual sense of false guilt from which Jesus Christ says we can be delivered entirely (Rom. 8:1).

Failure happens, but restoration is possible. Thank God for it and lead on.

QUESTIONS FOR REFLECTION

1. How do you feel when you admit a mistake or confess a sin? Are you able to resolve those feelings and move on?
2. What are some consequences leaders may face for leadership mistakes? Why is it hard to accept your consequences?
3. What is the difference between restoring a leader and sweeping problems under the rug?

Part Two

PRIORITIES FOR
ACTIVE LEADERS

INTRODUCTION

 Leaders are learners. We never stop growing, personally or professionally. We read books, listen to podcasts, attend seminars, and earn graduate degrees. We want the most information possible. Good leaders stay on the cutting edge, keep up with the times, and continually learn about their field. Leaders are insatiable, perpetual learners.

There comes a time, however, when the preparatory phase of learning is replaced by the priority of leading. The emphasis moves from gaining enough knowledge to lead at some future time to using what you now know to lead. Peter spent three years learning from Jesus. After that, it was time to lead. While he continued to learn new things, he was no longer focused on preparing to lead the church. He was now leading the church. Whether they felt ready or not, Jesus had ascended and told the Eleven to get moving. Peter had been trained to lead the disciples, and so he did. It was time for his natural leadership abilities, the principles he had learned from Jesus, and the skills he had practiced while serving with Jesus to come together for the good of others. It was time to lead. By considering what he did and how he did it, we can learn important insights for contemporary Christian leadership.

In part one, we asked the question, "What was Peter learning?" and discovered the leadership lesson in each story. In this section, we will again discern the big-picture idea from each story. The question for this section, however, is different. Now let's ask, "What was Peter doing?" While his specific actions are important, we will again look for the overarching principle. The Acts narrative and references in other New Testament books are foundational for understanding Peter's life and leadership in the early church.

Acts records many things that Peter did—for example, he preached about Jesus. A good commentary would dissect those sermons and analyze their content. For our purposes, the key insight is that Peter preached Jesus—not the particulars of how he preached Jesus. Rather than analyze the details (a worthwhile goal for other books), our focus is on what Peter's actions illustrate for Christian leaders of all time. These insights are informed by the particulars of the stories, but delving too deeply into them isn't necessary to reveal the broad principles underlying his leadership activities.

Some books advocate various "traits" of leaders. They imply that if you will simply implement the author's magic list, you will be a good leader. These leadership-trait theory books are helpful as long as they do not insist their list is the ultimate and final description of a capable leader. Regardless of how carefully crafted it might be, no list contains the complete formula for leading effectively. Other books identify leadership principles, skills, or practices like vision-casting or team-building as the supposed secrets to leadership effectiveness. While these examples, along with many other key functions are important, you should be similarly skeptical of any book purporting such a complete skills list. Again, this book makes no such claim. No one set of principles is the final word on Christian leadership. We will identify some key priorities for Christian leaders, but in no way are we claiming to exhaust the insights which might be needed for effective leadership. The principles illustrated by Peter's examples are important, but not comprehensive or exclusive.

What, then, makes the insights in this section important and helpful? Peter did some things that really mattered. His actions made a real difference. The stories about his leadership are so significant that they became Scripture. Therefore, his actions are priority actions for Christian leaders. More than just ancient incidents, they are models for ministry leadership for all time.

Emulating Peter will make you a better leader. His actions, while timely in their context, are also timeless in their application. Peter did what Christian leaders do. You may do more than he did, but you must not neglect doing what he did. Lead by starting with his example and adding to it as needed. Peter's actions aren't exclusive, but they are a great starting point for structuring your leadership priorities and activities.

You may find the actions described in this section surprising, partly because of their content, but also because of what's omitted. Leadership training materials today often focus on issues like the aforementioned vision-casting and team-building. They also highlight leading change, conflict resolution, mission focus, and a host of other activities. While these are important subjects (you can find some of these in my other books), perhaps too much credence has been given to them. Studying what a biblical leader did at a crucial time in the life of the church has challenged some of my assumptions about the foundations of Christian leadership. It has changed some of my convictions and reshaped my classroom teaching notes. Learning what Peter did as a leader will hopefully change your priorities about what you do that truly makes a difference.

My goal in this section is to ferret out leadership insights by asking, "What was Peter doing?" and more broadly, "What is the overarching principle about leadership revealed by what Peter did as a leader in Acts?" To reiterate, this book isn't a full commentary on the texts describing Peter's actions. While studying those texts has been foundational to finding the leadership insights contained in this section, presenting exegetical details isn't my goal. The stories in Acts deserve detailed study and you would profit by doing it. Perhaps the following short chapters will whet your appetite for more in-depth consideration of the Acts narratives.

Our purpose here is discerning what leaders do today that makes a difference by considering the example of a significant biblical leader. Doing this will reveal *some* traits and *some* practices of Christian leaders. While not a comprehensive list, they are certainly priority actions of capable leaders. By studying a biblical leader, you will be able to discern timeless truths about what leaders do that really matters. What Peter did as the most prominent leader selected by Jesus is an example for church and ministry leaders for all time. He's an important model, but certainly not the only model. Peter's also a unique model because his learning phase and his leading phase are both detailed in Scripture. This allows for some correlation not possible with other leaders whose leadership seasons aren't described as fully in the Bible.

This section continues the pattern of laying out one key leadership insight per chapter from each major story in Acts or the Epistles about

Peter. At the end of each chapter, there are reflection questions to help you personalize this material. There's also a question to help you connect the leadership priorities in this section to the leadership lessons in section one. Reviewing those lessons and thinking about their connections to these leadership priorities can reinforce both principles in your life. The following chapters are about what Peter did, and what you can do, to make a genuine difference where you are leading right now.

While Peter's life doesn't illustrate every important leadership lesson there is to learn, his prominence in the Bible demands we study him. While no single individual's leadership example is comprehensive and exclusive, the insights gained from studying Peter are wide-ranging enough for global appeal and specific enough for personal application in every ministry setting. He is only one model—but a significant model for contemporary ministry leadership.

Leaders learn from other leaders. Let's get started learning what Peter models about Christian leadership today.

TAKE THE LEAD

Acts 1:12–26

 Leaders take the lead. This may seem like stating the obvious, but it's actually the foundational statement about what leaders do. Leaders lead. They stand up, step forward, and assume responsibility for helping other people get something done. A military officer told me that the first rule when placed in command is, "Command."

Leaders, even when they are young, recognize when something is disorganized, underperforming, or needs help to move forward. When my oldest son, a born leader if there ever was one, was about six, he accompanied me to a speaking engagement. When we arrived, a large crowd of people was milling about, talking and laughing like people do when they are waiting for something to start. We didn't know anyone, so I was scanning the crowd, looking for the person in charge. My son tugged on my jacket. When I looked down, he asked, "Who's the boss of this?" The clear implication: if no one was in charge, he was willing to take over as needed.

Leaders are people who, if parachuted into any situation, spontaneously start strategizing how to make it better. They can't help it—leading is in their blood. While everyone can learn leadership skills, some people are born with the leadership gene. Natural-born leaders become more skilled through training, but their inborn tendencies are a gift from God. They are created to lead and find their greatest fulfillment in doing so. Leaders take the lead. It's what they do.

Peter had been a leader long before he'd met Jesus. He'd built a commercial fishing business with multiple boats and business partners as an expression of his abilities. When Jesus selected him, it wasn't surprising that he quickly became the central figure among the original disciples. He is always mentioned first in any list of the Twelve, as well as first in any mention of the inner core with James and John. The Gospels record more direct interaction between Jesus and Peter than between Jesus and the other disciples combined. Peter was a leader before he became one of the Twelve, and he was the leader among the Twelve.

It was only natural, then, for Peter to assume leadership of the embryonic church after Jesus' ascension. The Eleven, minus Judas, of course, made their way to an upper room where they had been staying together. The disciples had been meeting regularly for prayer with several women, including Mary (Jesus' mother), and Jesus' brothers. In total, 120 believers formed the group. With Jesus ascended and his commission ringing in their ears, they needed to decide what to do next.

Peter took the lead. One biblical phrase subtly communicates his emergence in this role: Peter "stood up among the brothers." While this might seem like a literary device, not a description of physical movement, it was probably both. Either way, Peter took the lead. He stood up. He took a stand. He stepped to the front and began moving the church toward fulfilling the commission Jesus had given them.

Peter's first message to the church was brief, yet specific. He referenced how Scripture was fulfilled by Judas' treachery and its ultimate results—his suicidal death and lonely burial. Peter then called for the selection of a replacement disciple to round out the Twelve. This was particularly important from his perspective, so there would be twelve eyewitnesses to the resurrection. The replacement needed to come from among believers who had followed the Lord for an extended time period—from John's baptism through Jesus' resurrection.

Two men—Joseph and Matthias—were nominated. The church prayed and cast lots (meaning they drew stones from a bag or some other means of random selection) to determine God's will. Matthias was selected and became the newest member of the Twelve, one of the leading witnesses to the life, death, and most important, the resurrection of Jesus. Peter had accomplished his first leadership goal. The way he did it reveals much about sound leadership practices for ministry leaders today.

Peter took responsibility for moving the church forward, summarized the background of the situation and the reasons change was needed, referenced Scripture to support his actions, and shared his opinion about how the church should proceed. He then engaged the church's participation in the nomination and selection process and guided the church to implement its ultimate conclusion. In the first example of church leadership in the Bible, the process Peter followed is an insightful model for leading churches in almost any situation. Let's expand on these steps—what it means when a leader takes the lead in a church or ministry organization. But first, let's underscore what taking the lead does not mean.

When a leader takes the lead, it does not mean domination or dictatorship. It doesn't mean you lead by fiat or with authority you haven't earned in the situation. Christian leadership isn't bombastic, intimidating, or heavy-handed. Taking the lead doesn't mean taking over, controlling others, or manipulating outcomes. Christian leadership isn't autocratic order-giving. It's a complex process modeled by Peter in his first leadership experience, and it's one you can learn to work through to a successful conclusion.

Leaders take initiative and assume responsibility for finding solutions. Taking initiative for solving problems, however, isn't the same as taking over a situation. Leaders aren't satisfied with the status quo and don't accept the conclusion that things can't be improved. Peter believed it was important to appoint a new disciple, but he didn't appoint the disciple. He identified the problem and called the church together to solve it.

Leaders inform their followers about their situation; they give appropriate information that will lead to informed decisions. Peter summarized the situation the church was facing. He gave them pertinent background information that would motivate them to take action. Information, shared in the right context, is a leader's friend. When most people have the facts, they will draw reasonable conclusions. Leadership often involves communicating information and letting the facts speak for themselves.

Leaders use the Bible appropriately to support their actions. When the Bible speaks clearly on an issue, Christian leaders stand firmly on those instructions. But many issues that churches and ministries must face aren't so clear cut. These might include personnel choices, building program options, and ministry programming possibilities. There's seldom a biblical right or wrong on these issues. Wise leaders, however, use the Bible to guide decision-making by drawing relevant principles from Scripture and applying them appropriately.

Peter did this in shaping the church's understanding of the reason for his request that they select a replacement disciple. Proof-texting and "God-told-me-so" uses of the Bible are out of bounds. Using the Bible to leverage your opinion or dictate outcomes is unethical. Using it appropriately, however, is essential for sound leadership.

Leaders share their perspective or counsel on ministry decisions. While taking the lead doesn't mean dictating outcomes, the opposite extreme is also unhelpful. As the leader, your counsel and judgment matter. You are guiding a group forward, not just waiting on them to decide an issue and then doing whatever they say. Your voice matters a great deal as you fulfill your God-given calling. Peter gave his counsel about what the church should do. While he didn't control the outcome, he influenced it strongly by establishing the parameters for making the choice. Giving counsel based on your professional experience and training is an important part of taking the lead.

Leaders engage their followers in leadership processes. This takes different forms depending on the type of church government or ministry procedures you must navigate. Even in hierarchical organizations and cultures, there's still value in gathering information from followers, gaining insight from their perspective, and drawing on their wisdom before a decision is made. Engaging followers, coworkers, and others in decision-making processes doesn't diminish your leadership authority. It increases your influence because people feel they are valued—not just as donors to or implementers of your plans—but as full ministry partners. Peter invited nominations, in the context of the established parameters, for the replacement disciple. He included the church in the leadership process.

Leaders guide the implementation of decisions, projects, and programs. While leaders often focus on casting vision and moving people toward general goals, part of taking the lead is making sure plans are executed. The more senior your leadership role, the larger the projects and the longer they take to implement. Peter had a relatively short implementation—getting Matthias named among the Twelve as witness to the resurrection. You may face much larger, long-term challenges. Nevertheless, leaders do more than generate ideas and hope they are approved. Leaders take the lead until the job gets done.

QUESTIONS FOR REFLECTION

1. What does it mean to "take the lead?" Are you reluctant to do this?
2. Which of the steps involved in taking the lead outlined in this chapter are most difficult for you? Why?
3. Why do some Christian leaders struggle with being too controlling or authoritarian in their leadership functions? How are you handling this problem?
4. Which leadership lessons (from the first section) prepare you to take the lead?

Priority 2

TELL THE TRUTH

Acts 2:14–36

 Pentecost happened! The church gathered for worship, and the Holy Spirit made his dramatic appearance. There was a sound like a rushing wind, flames of fire above the believers' heads, and various languages coming from their mouths as a result of the filling of the Spirit. People heard the gospel in multiple languages, simultaneously, as people from many nations marveled at the Galileans gone global. Nothing like this had ever happened before, so groping for an explanation was only natural. Some observers were moved deeply, perplexed and reflective about what it all might mean. Others, not so much. Their conclusion was far less spiritual: the speakers were just falling down drunk.

Someone needed to step forward and clarify the situation, to define the events in spiritual terms simple and direct enough for all to understand.

Peter once again "stood up with the Eleven," raising his voice to explain what was happening. In the midst of significant confusion—both practical and theological—Peter told the truth. He told the truth about what was happening and why. He told the truth about God's activity in the moment. He told the truth about what it meant for those impacted by the events. Peter stood up, stepped forward, and defined reality in the situation. Leaders tell the truth, and they let the truth do its life-changing, sin-confronting, controversy-causing work among the people.

Peter began by confronting the rumor that believers were drunk. He explained the phenomena being observed as originating in Old Testament prophecy. He quoted a biblical passage from Joel and applied it to the situation. There was a reasonable, scriptural explanation for what was happening, and Peter wanted that emphasized. He did not want some speculative, humanistic explanation to eliminate the supernatural aspect of the events.

Then Peter expanded his message to summarize the life, death, and resurrection of Jesus—the ultimate power source for the Pentecostal events. Peter was particularly clear about his hearers' responsibility for Jesus' death. He said, "You used lawless people to nail Him to a cross and kill Him" and "God has made this Jesus, whom you crucified, both Lord and Messiah!" You can't be much more direct than that. Peter communicated the truth about Jesus and the responsibility people have to respond to him, no matter how confrontational it might sound. Peter quoted several additional Old Testament prophecies to validate the truth of his message.

Peter also used his message to establish the centrality of the resurrection, elevating Jesus' stature in the minds of those who very recently had seen him crucified and buried. Those hearers would have readily accepted the facts of Jesus' death and burial. They had seen those events. The resurrection, however, was another matter. Not everyone there had seen the resurrected Jesus, but Peter and the Eleven were the primary witnesses and they were determined to tell the story. Leaders tell the truth—even truth almost too impossible to believe—and they call people to live with its implications.

Peter also told the truth to correct a misconception about his fellow leaders and believers. Their critics were deriding them as drunkards. Peter explained that their behavior was a result of being Spirit-filled. This was a remarkable explanation—both for its audacity and its uniqueness. While those experiencing the phenomena may have remembered some Old Testament reference to ecstatic behavior prompted by God's Spirit, none of them had ever experienced or seen anything like what was happening. Peter's explanation did two things. First, it stamped out a rumor that would have embarrassed the early church and undermined the power of the Pentecostal miracles. Second, it established a supernatural explanation for unusual or remarkable events in the life of the church. As a leader, you must define and explain God's activity so your followers understand when God is at work and when he isn't. This kind of discernment is required for Christian leaders.

A ministry was experiencing amazing financial success. Over a period of six months, several million dollars in gifts flowed into the work. The members were grateful. The leaders celebrated the success but reminded their followers that the results were from God's miraculous provision, not just the result of careful fund-raising. The leaders traced the onset of the financial blessings to a decision they had made some months earlier to be more generous with the ministry's resources. Trusting God's promises to provide generously for them, they had been giving away their resources to help other ministries—not enough to jeopardize their mission, but enough to be a sacrifice for the good of others. The leaders told the truth about God keeping his word to bless generous givers—even organizational givers—and made sure the explanation for what had happened focused on God's supernatural activity. Leaders help followers make the spiritual connections needed to keep the focus on him.

Peter told the truth by connecting the Bible to life events. He offered a perspective on what was happening based on Scripture. He referenced ultimate Truth in telling the truth about a contemporary situation. He made application of truth in a practical way, explaining God's perspective on human events. Christian leaders must be skilled in using the Bible to provide context and meaning for complex life situations. Doing so is a mark of maturity and humility—you know enough to know you don't know enough to give counsel apart from Scripture.

Leaders deal with complex situations. The more senior your leadership role, the more complicated the situations will be. After all, if the problem was simple, someone else in the organization would have likely resolved it. Solomon-like "babies" are the only kind of problems presented to you. There's often not a single Bible verse or passage that speaks to these kinds of complicated issues. Leaders must be able to use the Bible, like Peter did, interweaving texts to create a composite answer for thorny, complicated situations.

Peter also told the truth by witnessing about what he had personally observed. He told about the resurrection—not as a theory but as an eyewitness. Telling the truth means you testify to your experience with God. You aren't ashamed of his activity in your life and what you have learned through walking with Him. When you do this, you help people understand how God works today—revealing himself and working directly with people. Telling the truth, like a witness in a courtroom, means sharing your story. It means boldly telling others, without shame, apology, or reticence, how God has intervened in your life. Doing this in a postmodern world is a powerful testimony to others who long to experience the supernatural. When you report your experiences, it encourages others to seek God and expect similar results.

Sharing your story of personally meeting Jesus falls into this category. When you report your encounter with the resurrected Jesus, you join a long line of Christian witnesses going back to the newly formed Twelve who spoke up at Pentecost. While you may not be skilled in using Scripture to validate the resurrection, you can tell the story of how the living Lord Jesus has come into your life. There's really no argument against a changed life. As a leader, your personal story of meeting the resurrected Jesus is compelling. When you tell the truth about how Jesus has changed you, your story rings with clarity and authenticity.

Telling the truth involves standing up and speaking up. It means accurately reporting God's activity in today's world. Telling the truth means aligning your comments with the Bible and using scriptural insight to explain life situations. When you tell the truth about Jesus, you witness about his death, burial, and resurrection. Telling the truth is more than reciting historical facts. It's telling people about a living Lord.

Leaders tell the truth—even when it's controversial or confrontational. We tell the truth about our experiences with God. We tell the truth winsomely, but recognize that truth and Truth create their own tension. Helping people resolve that tension is also a leadership responsibility.

QUESTIONS FOR REFLECTION

1. Why is it hard to tell the truth?
2. Why is it difficult to interweave scriptural insights into leading people? How can you improve this skill?
3. Do you value your story of God's work in your life as truth that can transform other people? If not, why not?
4. Which leadership lessons prepare you to tell the truth?

Priority 3

CALL PEOPLE TO JESUS

Acts 2:37–40

In today's laissez-faire, tolerance-for-everyone, all-beliefs-are-the-same kind of world, Christian leaders call people to Jesus. We challenge people to live for higher purposes, to give themselves for the greater good. We confront tolerance, accommodation, and other high-sounding "values" for what they really are—masked selfishness. Calling for commitment is more than just talking people into doing good things. It starts with demanding that they turn from their sinful self-absorption. It culminates in directing them to submit to Jesus as Lord. When a person does this for the first time, conversion happens. Subsequent submission experiences contribute to sanctification. Christian leaders call people to Jesus. If we don't, who will?

Peter minced no words the first time someone asked how to respond to the message about Jesus. The crowds had heard the gospel preached in their native languages by the apostles and other believers at Pentecost. Then they heard Peter's subsequent message about the death, burial, and resurrection of Jesus. Peter was very direct in his message. He assigned responsibility for the death of Jesus to those who were listening to him at that moment. There was no putting off of responsibility to the Jews or Romans who actually did the deed. They were merely viewed as agents for the real perpetrators—his hearers. Peter concluded his message by declaring that Jesus was both Lord and Messiah.

The response of the crowd was prompted by deep conviction about their sin of abusing Jesus. "Coming under conviction" is a phrase that has virtually passed from the contemporary Christian lexicon. The phrase means being willfully broken, bereft of pride, and confounded by one's depravity. It means you see yourself as the sinner you are, and you are repulsed. Deep conviction means you are moved profoundly and ready to make serious spiritual changes. It can involve an emotional experience with expressions of grief like weeping or crying out to God. It is more than an emotional response, however. It cuts to the core of who you are and prompts you to make real changes.

Faking contrition is a cheap substitute for genuine conviction of sin. Manipulating emotional response to validate ministry is unethical. Don't let concerns for cheapening the process, however, rob you of its benefits. Telling the truth about Jesus, about the sin of rejecting him, and about the disastrous consequences of failing to change should prompt deep conviction. When we ignore this spiritual dynamic or try to conjure it up by fleshly effort, we miss out on the precursor to real spiritual change—the conviction of sin.

When the crowds came under conviction, they cried out, "What must we do?" Peter gave a direct answer, the only answer that truly resolves deep conviction over sin. He told them to repent (personal change) and be baptized (public evidence of change). Repentance means reversing course and turning back from sin. Being baptized was a bold public declaration resulting from repentance.

Peter continued, reminding them that repentance leads to the forgiveness of sin and reception of the Holy Spirit. Their baptism was made in the name of Jesus Christ—a public confession of their commitment to the Lord. Peter's entire message isn't recorded. The Bible says he spoke "many other words" including the admonition to be saved from the corruption of their generation. No doubt he covered many implications of their new commitment to Jesus. His central theme—however controversial and confrontational—was for them to repent from sin and follow Jesus. All spiritual life starts there.

Christian leaders call people to repent of their sins, to place their faith in Jesus, and to publicly confess their new allegiance through baptism. At the crucial moment of the birth of the church, Peter's message is both an example and a motivation. His message is an example because it reminds us of the core message, foundational to the founding and continuity of the church. We must communicate that message to every generation. It's motivational because we see the dramatic impact the gospel has on the deepest need of humankind—forgiveness of sin and creation of new life in Jesus.

If the gospel is our core message and calling people to repent of their sins is the first response, how are we doing? If baptism is the essential public confession of faith, how important is it today?

Many leaders have abandoned simply preaching the gospel and anticipating that the Holy Spirit will convict of sin. They seldom specifically call people to repentance or give them the opportunity for public response (leading to baptism). Leaders who make this choice have bought into the myths that preaching must be needs-driven, seeker-friendly, PowerPoint-illustrated, and delivered in a casual, nonaggressive way. Further, according to this way of thinking, a good sermon offers options more than it seeks to persuade.

There is some truth to this method. Some preaching should focus on personal issues like parenting or stewardship. All preaching should be seeker-accessible, meaning anyone can understand the vocabulary and follow the reasoning. Using visual support like video or projected slides can be helpful. A preacher's tone should be winsome, not repellent. But the spiritual power to change a person's eternal destiny isn't connected to any of these stylistic choices.

Many modern leaders have allowed these methods to supplant preaching the gospel. When gospel preaching, including the call for commitment to Jesus, is neglected by church leaders (no matter how positive the reasons might sound), the church is neutered of its core lifesaving, eternally significant message—the gospel.

The problem also shows up in contemporary evangelism strategies. The deceptive phrase "share the gospel; use words if necessary" undercuts both the biblical pattern and practical reality of how people understand the gospel. If you think your holy, loving lifestyle will convert others without a verbal proclamation, think again. Not even Jesus himself could make that strategy work. He lived a perfect life but still had to explain what it meant to believe in and follow him. Many Christians, even leaders, are reluctant to tell another person about Jesus and ask them to become his follower. They adopt the gospel song, "They will know we are Christians by his love" as their evangelism strategy. It's true: The Bible teaches that unbelievers will know we are Christians by our love, but they won't know *how to become a Christian* by our love. They won't know how to become a Christian unless someone tells them the gospel.

Leaders must resist these deceptive practices; we must overcome our cowardice and model courage about our message. We must resist substituting spiritually soft preaching for the gospel. Our personal witnessing must be about Jesus—not some self-help or life-improvement program. We must boldly challenge people to follow Jesus, asking them to make a genuine commitment to him.

We must also reclaim our understanding of baptism—believer's baptism by immersion—as the primary means of public confession of faith. As a Baptist, this seems natural to me. Even some Baptist leaders, however, now minimize the importance of baptism. This is rooted in a reticence to confront people about Jesus and the gospel. They want to minimize barriers to identification as a Christian and make it easier to become part of a church. Doing so, however, diminishes the power of public confession and, in the long run, undermines our collective public witness of the gospel. If a person won't be baptized among supportive believers, how will they ever openly share the gospel among their non-Christian friends?

One pastor recognized this drift in his ministry and decided to do something radical. In the early morning worship service of his church, he preached a gospel message explaining baptism as evidence of belief. He invited people to be baptized on the spot. In a service attended by two hundred, more than forty came forward and asked to be immediately immersed. Several asked if they could be baptized after the second service and then left to retrieve family and friends to see them baptized. The pastor repeated the same invitation in the second service. All told, ninety-six people were baptized that day.

This example doesn't mean every church should practice immediate baptism every week or even very often. All it illustrates is the pent-up desire people have for public response. They attend polite, well-structured worship services week after week—but no one asks for public commitment. Christian faith is supposed to be lived openly, not secretly. It's a community faith, not just a personal experience. As a leader, don't believe the lie that asking people for commitment will turn them away from Christianity.

The opposite is true. People will publicly commit to something that really matters.

Call people to Jesus. Have the courage to share the gospel—both through preaching and personal evangelism—and to facilitate open identification as Jesus' followers. As a leader, you must be a model of gospel-centered communication. Your followers are counting on you and will draw strength from your example. Be bold.

QUESTIONS FOR REFLECTION

1. Why is it so hard to call people to repentance and faith in Jesus?
2. Are you giving appropriate emphasis to the gospel in your preaching and witnessing? If not, what needs to change?
3. Do you emphasize baptism as an important step of obedience to Jesus? Why or why not?
4. Which leadership lessons prepare you to call people to Jesus?

Priority 4

ACCESS GOD'S POWER

Acts 3:1–10; 5:12–16; 9:32–43

 Christian leaders must accomplish more than their abilities, skills, and training can produce. Often, we celebrate a leader's gifting when they lead well. But overconfidence in a leader's gifting is detrimental to overall effectiveness when they masquerade as personal, self-contained sources of power or influence. Christian leaders must access God's power for their work. There should be a sense of the supernatural, an aura of mystery around what we do. Our achievements should be measured beyond what can be explained by human ingenuity.

There are three distinct stories about Peter's leadership that reveal God's power working through him. God apparently wanted multiple references to supernatural power moving through Peter to be part of the Acts narrative. Putting these three incidents together recognizes their commonality. Combining them underscores the importance of this principle: spiritual leaders access God's power.

Peter and John were headed to the temple to pray. They passed by a lame man who begged for a gift. Peter got his attention and told him, "I don't have silver or gold, but what I have, I give you: In the name of Jesus Christ the Nazarene, get up and walk!" Peter then helped him to his feet, and the formerly lame man started leaping around, praising God. He accompanied Peter into the temple where people looked on with awe and amazement. This was a powerful demonstration of God's power moving through a leader to bring healing.

This wasn't the only time Peter was instrumental in healing someone. Sometime later, in Lydda, Peter visited a paralyzed man named Aeneas. He had been bedridden for eight years until Peter announced, "Jesus Christ heals you." Aeneas got up, made his bed, and celebrated his healing by spreading the word about Jesus in his community. As a result, many people turned to the Lord.

Peter was recognized as a man with special access to God's power. The apostles in Jerusalem were held in high esteem, none more than Peter. Word spread about his healing power. People would carry the sick and lame into the streets and lay them on cots, hoping that when Peter walked by, his shadow would touch them. While there's no record of any shadow healings, these actions reveal the reverence people had for the apostles and their recognition of the spiritual power moving through them. Peter was well-known as a channel through which God accomplished supernatural results.

All these healings were trumped, however, by what Peter did in Joppa. A beloved widow, Dorcas, had died. Peter went to her bedside, prayed, and called her back to life. This was his most dramatic miracle, a resuscitation of a person cherished by the church.

Christian leadership is supernatural leadership. You trust God to work through you to accomplish more than your talents, abilities, skills, and training can produce. How does this happen, and what does it look like today?

Leaders must magnify Jesus and access his power for supernatural leadership results. Peter told the lame man outside the temple to get up "in the name of Jesus." He later announced to Aeneas, "Jesus heals you." The starting point for accessing supernatural power is recognizing that Jesus has all power and authority in the universe. Confessing this reality is one thing; actually humbling yourself on a daily basis and submitting to Jesus is quite another. Leaders can easily become enamored with their abilities—"delusions of adequacy," one friend calls it. When Peter encountered lameness, he didn't say, "because of my superior intellectual training, you may now get up and walk." Peter called on Jesus to exercise *his* power to do something humanly impossible. You access spiritual power for leadership by submitting yourself to Jesus, praying in his name, speaking his name as the centerpiece of your message, and trusting Jesus to work through and around you in response to your submission to him.

Does this mean you will see dramatic results on an everyday basis? Probably not. Peter led the church for years, with only a few healings recorded in Acts. This doesn't mean there weren't other healings. There may have been; we just don't know. Acts is a selective history, recording significant moments and turning points in early church history.

It isn't a comprehensive story. It's likely the apostles had many routine days of preaching, teaching, meeting human needs, and solving church problems—coupled with dramatic days when an unusual healing or other miracle took place. Your ministry may follow this pattern and still have the touch of the supernatural about it.

Supernatural leadership involves God giving you strength to persevere in difficult times, provision to make it through lean times, and wisdom to counsel people through life's complex situations. You know that God is working when you hear words coming out of your mouth and you wonder, "Where did that idea or insight come from?"—even while you are saying it. You know God is working when you pray for money for a ministry project or personal need—and the money shows up. You know God is working when you are emotionally spent but you make one more home visit—and a person commits his life to Jesus.

These examples avoid the tougher question: Does God still work through Christian leaders to accomplish dramatic results like those in Acts? My answer: Yes. While these events don't happen daily (neither did they necessarily happen every day in the Acts era), there are serendipitous moments when God moves so powerfully that everyone is in awe at his intervention.

I was present when a dying man was healed and walked out of a hospital thirty-six hours after being told there was no hope. He lived a healthy and vigorous life for many additional years. I was present when an offering was received that exceeded all projected or dreamed of capabilities of the congregation. The offering was talked about for years as a pinnacle moment in that church's history. I was present when God invaded a worship service, his presence so strong dozens of people fell on their faces in repentance and prayer. The results were more than momentary catharsis. Church healing ensued. I was present when a philandering rebel confessed his sins to God and his wife. Years later, their marriage has been healed and their family demonstrates God grace.

God works in special moments, astounding us with his power and reminding us of our weakness in contrast. As a leader, you access God's power for routine responsibilities. You also ask God to break through in impossible situations and then cooperate with him when he does. Christian leaders must not quench the Spirit, but be prepared to recognize an authentic divine intervention and facilitate the response of their followers. You must also have the spiritual discipline and integrity to reject all attempts at manufacturing so-called holy moments. Fakery is an insult to God and destroys your integrity as a leader. Genuine openness to God's supernatural intervention (and spiritually responsive leadership when it happens) must be your goal.

A genuine divine intervention always has one or both of these two results: God is glorified, and people are saved. When these moments occur, part of their validation and authentication as being from God is whether or not people are awed at God's power and drawn to faith in Jesus. These are the two primary results in these stories about Peter. They are the same results associated with the other miracle stories in Acts. Any lesser outcome cheapens the experience and turns the attention back to human ingenuity. Wise leaders recognize God at work and focus their attention, and the attention of their followers, on glorifying God and gathering followers for Jesus.

As a leader, you are expected to be a person who accesses God's power—a conduit through which God works to accomplish more than you can do in your own strength. Be this kind of leader. Don't be afraid of God's supernatural intervention. Ask him to reveal his power through you in so-called routine tasks, and around you in dramatic demonstrations of spiritual strength. Cooperate with him in both instances, ready to show the essence of true Christian leadership—dependence on God and deference to Him—when he acts.

QUESTIONS FOR REFLECTION

1. Why must Christian leaders access God's power for true success?
2. When have you experienced God's power through your leadership?
3. What should a Christian leader do when God dramatically intervenes through them or around them?
4. Which leadership lessons prepare you to access God's power?

Priority 5

MAGNIFY JESUS

Acts 3:11–26

 A family once visited our church for the first time. After the service, during a casual conversation, I discovered the woman in the family was Jewish. Linda had never attended a Christian worship service and seemed fascinated by what she had just experienced. I followed up with a personal phone call a few days later. She accepted my offer of a pastoral visit with her and her husband. Having limited experience with Jewish guests—not many drop in on a typical Midwestern Baptist church—I spent some time thinking about how to open the conversation in their home. Based on our prior conversation from Sunday, I settled on a question that received a surprising, but delightful answer.

My question was, "What was the biggest difference between our worship service and the synagogue services you've experienced in the past?" Linda said, "Oh that's easy. In your church, Jesus is the 'Big One.'" I had never heard it put quite that way before. Having worshipped God all her life, it was striking to her how prominent Jesus was in our worship. We sang about Jesus, prayed in Jesus' name, and talked about how Jesus could change lives. Jesus was mentioned multiple times in the sermon. Linda's comment came with a twinkle in her eye. She was bemused, but obviously observant and intrigued. I took her comment as a compliment.

When Peter healed the lame man outside the temple, it stirred quite a response. The man followed Peter and John into the temple, leaping and praising God for his healing. This attracted a crowd. The beggar was well-known; seeing him healed was quite a sight. People ran to see the results of the miracle firsthand. A crowd gathered, staring at the apostles and marveling at the miracle wrought by their hands.

Peter could sense what was happening. He and John were about to be credited for the healing. Later in Acts, Paul would be called a god because of his proximity to a miracle. Perhaps Peter sensed the same conclusion about to be drawn. To ward off such nonsense, he asked the crowd two probing questions, "Why are you amazed at this?" and "Why do you stare at us, as . . . though we had made him walk by our own power or godliness?"

Peter shifted the focus away from the apostles as agents of healing to the true Source of spiritual power. He proclaimed, "The God of Abraham, Isaac, and Jacob, the God of our fathers, has glorified His Servant Jesus." Peter seized the moment. The crowd, drawn by the miracle, needed firm leadership to direct their attention away from praising men to glorifying Jesus. Too many leaders seize a moment like this for the wrong purpose. God enables dramatic, successful ministry, and they celebrate their success, compliment followers for their assistance, and congratulate themselves on their ingenuity. Peter had the spiritual maturity and discipline to keep the focus on Jesus.

Peter then captured the moment for Jesus in another way. The miracle had attracted a crowd and created learning readiness for an explanation. Peter focused their attention on Jesus and preached a gospel-centered message calling them to commitment to the Lord. Like his previous message at Pentecost, Peter was again confrontational and direct about Jesus. He reminded the crowd of their responsibility for his death. He also reminded them of the prophecies fulfilled by Jesus' life, death, and resurrection. All that Peter preached was for their benefit. Jesus had come to turn them from evil and give them a quality of life found only in him.

Christian leaders magnify Jesus. It's his name we put up in lights. His fame, his renown is our priority. When good is done through us, we focus on his enabling grace—we don't congratulate ourselves for a job well done.

We praise Jesus, pray in the name of Jesus, challenge people to trust Jesus, sing about Jesus, and otherwise make him the centerpiece of our worship and work. Magnifying Jesus is difficult because of our propensity for taking credit when it's not deserved. It's also difficult because of the growing global animosity toward Jesus.

A few years ago, a secular youth organization asked me to pray before an international gathering. Having worked with their leaders on other projects, I was delighted for the honor and impressed that they included prayer in their gathering. The day after I agreed to participate, one of the organizers called to talk about my prayer. They were having second thoughts. They were concerned that my prayer would be controversial. He wanted me to know it was an eclectic gathering—so my prayer needed to be generic enough not to offend anyone.

My reply was gracious, but firm. "You're probably concerned that I will pray in the name of Jesus. Well, if you would like, I will quietly step aside. I am a Christian minister. That's how we pray—to Jesus. If you want a different kind of prayer, you need to ask a different religious leader." To his credit, the caller indicated his confidence in me to pray appropriately and retracted his concerns. I prayed—in the name of Jesus—without apology.

In our world, demeaning some religions or religious figures is cause for protests, riots, and violence. Christians, however, are chided for even praying in public in the name of Jesus. We are reviled for using the name of our Savior and Lord. Christian leaders who kowtow to this pressure may be leaders, but they will have forfeited the privilege of the adjectival modifier. They may be leaders but they are not truly *Christian* leaders. Christian leaders magnify the name of Jesus; we exalt him for his death, burial, and resurrection and praise him for the lives that are changed as a result.

Magnifying Jesus means more, however, than just praying in his name. It means making Jesus the center of our preaching; focusing on Jesus as the prominent part of our worship gatherings; communicating the message about Jesus' death, burial, and resurrection; and calling people to commit themselves to Jesus—not to a church or ministry organization. Magnifying Jesus means making him the centerpiece of your life and ministry leadership.

Leaders are competent people who have frequent success. But when you are successful, how do you keep the focus on Jesus, even while you acknowledge the good work of others and allow others to express gratitude to you?

First, remember that Jesus is the Source of everything good in your life. Your health, talents, abilities, skills, and even the good things you have learned from others—these all originated with Jesus. He has given you new life through conversion and real purpose for living by calling you to lead. Developing healthy humility that enables you to focus more on Jesus is foundational to naturally and frequently giving him glory.

Second, remember Jesus is the Source of any remarkable results in your ministry. If everything happening through you can be explained by the work of your two hands, something is wrong. When you see supernatural results, take no credit. Give Jesus glory for what he has done through you.

Third, express gratitude to your followers and to Jesus for your followers. By doing this, you shift the focus from what you have done to what Jesus has done through others. Remind yourself that your followers are Jesus' gift to you—they are members of his kingdom entrusted to you for guidance. Without followers, there are no leaders. Focusing on their contribution more than your leadership helps you magnify Jesus.

As a Christian leader, your attitude must reflect how John the Baptist described his relationship with Jesus: "He must increase, but I must decrease" (John 3:30). While people may appreciate your leadership, you want them to remember that you directed their attention to Jesus, not yourself. Stifling pride and self-promotion is hard, particularly when things go well. Make the hard choice—no matter how successful you become—to keep the right perspective. Magnify Jesus. Make him known. Make him famous. Honor his name now. It's his name we will be exalting for eternity. Jesus is the Big One, remember?

QUESTIONS FOR REFLECTION

1. Have you been pressured to avoid using the name of Jesus? How did you respond? How will you in the future?
2. How can you magnify Jesus more consistently in your ministry?
3. When you are tempted to take the credit for leadership success, what helps you resist that temptation?
4. Which leadership lessons prepare you to magnify Jesus?

Priority 6

OBEY GOD

Acts 4:1–22

 Leaders face pressure to conform to the expectations of others. People-pleasing and succumbing to peer pressure are real challenges—not just for teenagers but for everyone. My front yard had a huge brown spot. I tried everything to fix it. The problem was made worse by my neighbor across the street, "Mr. Better Homes and Gardens." His lawn was perfect. Exasperated by my failed attempts, I told my wife, "I'm calling a lawn service." The next day, while I was standing outside looking at my ugly lawn, my neighbor wandered over and said, "You've got a real problem here. You're not thinking about calling in some kind of lawn service, are you?"

Male ego, peer pressure, and some kind of weird horticultural pride all converged as these words came out of my mouth, "Nooooo—I can handle this." He smiled and said as he left, "That's what I hoped. A man should be able to take care of his own yard." For years, that silly conversation has echoed in my mind, reminding me how easy it is to give in to pleasing people. Many of us will do or say almost anything to look good in front of others. Leaders must break this destructive pattern because the stakes in their decisions are so significant.

Peter faced a much more serious situation than my ridiculous lawn. The healing of the lame man outside the temple, coupled with his preaching to the gathered crowd, had produced a throng of people repenting from sin and believing in Jesus. Over five thousand men were converted that day. What a chaotic scene it must have been! The temple leaders, particularly the high priest, weren't pleased. They took Peter and John into custody and jailed them overnight.

The next morning a coalition of rulers, elders, and priests—led by the high priest, Annas, and members of his family—gathered to investigate and punish the apostles. An interrogator asked, "By what power or in what name" they had accomplished the miracle and preached the subsequent sermon. The answer was obvious and probably already known to the inquisitors. How could anyone not know the answer, given the size and scope of the previous day's events? The name of Jesus had been prominent.

Peter answered the question with a short message summarizing the healing and the resulting conversions. He then preached the gospel, telling the assembled Jewish leaders about Jesus: "There is salvation in no one else, for there is no other name under heaven given to people, and we must be saved by it." Consider how courageous he was to make this infuriating statement to the temple leaders who regarded themselves as arbiters of the only proper way to a relationship with God.

The assembly was dumbfounded by the boldness of the preachers, the truth of the message, and—most pointedly—by the once lame man standing in their midst, fully healed. The Sanhedrin dismissed the apostles to consider their limited options. After all, the lame man was healed—no denying that. The preaching that resulted, however, was the larger problem. It had to be stopped. They came up with the best solution they could—they ordered Peter and John not to speak anymore in the name of Jesus. They threatened them with dire consequences if they disregarded this order. Given what had recently been done to Jesus, the apostles no doubt realized the gravity of their situation.

Peter faced a dilemma. He had two choices, both with potentially painful outcomes. He could obey the temple leaders, thus disappointing Jesus and his followers. Peter's personal pain and loss of leadership stature would have been significant. The other choice was to disobey the Sanhedrin's orders, likely resulting in physical punishment or death. Either way, it was going to be painful; pick your poison.

Peter articulated his choice clearly and immediately. He replied, "We are unable to stop speaking about what we have seen and heard." He prefaced this conclusion with the rhetorical statement, "Whether it's right in the sight of God for us to listen to you rather than to God, you decide." In plain terms, Peter announced he would obey God rather than men. He would continue to preach about Jesus, no matter the consequences. This confounded the Sanhedrin. They were afraid to punish the apostles because of their popularity and the number of people aware of the proceedings. So, they threatened them further and released them.

Leaders must have the courage to make the same decision Peter made—to obey God rather than man. Christian leaders face three kinds of opposition today—pressure, harassment, and persecution.

Pressure. Pressure is usually verbal or written attacks designed to embarrass, shame, humiliate, or manipulate a leader into a particular course of action. This may take many forms—from e-mail attacks to verbal altercations to power games (like a person threatening to stop giving to your ministry if you don't do what he or she wants).

Harassment. Harassment takes opposition to another level. It involves physical threats, financial penalties, and delaying tactics designed to prevent a leader or organization from accomplishing its Christian mission. One ministry attempted to develop property it owned, only to be thwarted by governmental opposition in the form of endless foot-dragging on their application, onerous extra fees demanded throughout the process, and surprising policy changes as the project unfolded. Millions of dollars were lost in the process.

Persecution. Persecution, the most intense form of opposition, involves physical attack on a leader resulting in illness, disability, or even death. Many Christian leaders around the world face these threats on a regular basis. One of my friends, for example, has been interrogated at gunpoint on numerous occasions, his captors trying to convince him to stop preaching the gospel. The Bible promises that persecution will intensify in the future.

Standing up to any level of opposition requires courage based on the choice to obey God, no matter the consequences. Developing this kind of courage isn't easy, but is essential for effective leadership. What motivated Peter, and what can motivate you to make this difficult choice?

You can be motivated by gratitude to God for the changes he has brought to your life. Through Jesus, he saved you from sin and called you into leadership. In profound appreciation for what he has done for you, determine to honor him with your leadership choices. A college student once explained why he was making good moral choices. He said, "I respect my father so much, I don't want to disappoint him." It's a privilege to have such a healthy relationship with a natural father. Not everyone does. But everyone can have a similar relationship with our heavenly Father. Determine to honor him with your choices because of your respect for him. Peter did this, in spite of the threats from people who supposedly knew God better than anyone.

You can be motivated by the power of God demonstrated through your ministry. By the time this story happened, Peter had experienced the miracles of Pentecost and the healing of the lame man. He had also seen thousands of people saved through his preaching—more than three thousand at Pentecost and more than five thousand following the healing outside the temple. Peter had seen God in action through his ministry in the name of Jesus. He wasn't going to renounce his allegiance to God, even to escape persecution, if it meant forfeiting the opportunity to access continued spiritual power. You must make the same choice. Don't sacrifice the privilege of God's power working through you. Don't give in just to lessen the pressure to conform. Stay the course. Continuing to experience God's power in your ministry is worth it.

You can also be motivated by the needs of people. When Peter looked at the healed man and thousands of new converts, he knew it was worth whatever price necessary to have those results. Your followers, but more important, the people in your community who aren't yet followers of Jesus, are depending on you to remain loyal to God and the gospel. Your faithfulness is essential for many reasons. Without effective Christian leaders, there's no hope for most people to be saved, to have their lives fulfilled or their families made whole, or to experience a host of other positive outcomes only possible through Jesus. For the sake of those who still need to hear the gospel, stand firm. When you do, a distinctive opportunity to experience authentic Christianity will be available in your community. Obey God rather than man.

QUESTIONS FOR REFLECTION

1. When have you obeyed man rather than God? How did it turn out in the end? What should you have done differently?
2. Are you experiencing pressure, harassment, or persecution? If so, how are you handling it?
3. Which of the motivators in this chapter helps you have the courage to obey God rather than man? How does it help you?
4. Which leadership lessons prepare you to obey God?

Priority 7

CONFRONT SIN

Acts 4:36–5:11; 8:14–25

 One of the hardest leadership tasks is confronting sinful behavior. Prophets speak out against cultural depravity and national rebellion against God. That's tough enough. Even more difficult is holding the line against sinful behavior by church members, employees of Christian ministries, or other leaders on your team. It's amazing what Christian leaders must confront to preserve ecclesiastical and/or ministerial integrity.

Two couples came forward in a worship service and announced they were getting divorces, switching spouses, and remarrying. "God had told them" to correct their mistake of choosing the wrong partners in the first place. They were shocked when church leaders denied their request for the church's blessing on their decision—after all, they had prayed about it.

A couple got married. The husband started an extramarital affair while on his honeymoon. Months later, he impregnated his mistress and the whole situation became public. His church's leaders confronted him—taking appropriate disciplinary action, supporting his wife (who became his ex-wife), and reaching out to the mistress and the child she soon bore.

A prominent ministry leader had a long-term affair. When it was discovered, he was dismissed from his leadership position. Rather than cooperate with a disciplinary process, he initiated legal action against his former employer. Holding him accountable in a public process proved almost impossible.

A pastor stole money from his church by falsifying his expense reports. The deacons eventually discovered what was happening, confronted him, and led the church to dismiss him from office. He fought them, claiming the church owed him extra compensation for overworking him during a recent building program.

Shall we go on? Christians aren't perfect. They sin, sometimes so egregiously that their actions bring disrepute on the church and must be confronted. Leaders also sin and must be confronted when their actions are unethical, illegal, immoral, or otherwise violate the sacred trust they have been given. Practicing church discipline or appropriate supervision in ministry organizations requires wisdom, good judgment, and courage. It's never an easy process; seldom a clean one. Nevertheless, Christian leaders must wade into ugly situations and muck out the mess sin leaves behind.

Peter faced two such situations that required taking a firm stand to preserve the church's integrity. The first involved a married couple, Ananias and Sapphira. A church leader named Barnabas sold some property and gave the money to the church. Ananias did the same, but held back part of the proceeds and gave the balance to the church. He created the impression he was giving the full amount like Barnabas had, but actually lied about the gift. Sapphira was fully aware of his duplicity and would pay a high price for her involvement.

When Peter learned of Ananias' deception, he confronted him. He called him out for what he had done, placed full responsibility on Ananias for his actions, and reminded him that he had lied to God, not just to the church. Upon hearing these words, Ananias dropped dead in his tracks. Three hours later, Sapphira arrived, not knowing what had happened to her husband. Peter quizzed her about the situation and discovered her involvement. Like her husband, when confronted by Peter, she also died. The result: great fear came upon the church. Holiness restored meant holiness expected.

Later, in Samaria, Peter was part of confirming the legitimacy of conversion among the Samaritans. The Holy Spirit filled them through laying on hands by the apostles. A man named Simon saw this and wanted the same power. He offered money to buy the ability to facilitate the Spirit's filling. Peter confronted him immediately. He told Simon his money could perish with him because his heart wasn't right with God. Peter challenged him to repent of his wicked behavior, to forsake the bitterness motivating such a perverted request, and to ask God to purify his motives. Simon responded humbly to the rebuke, pleading with Peter to pray for him "so that nothing you have said may happen to me." Simon understood the possible consequences of his actions and turned from them.

In both these situations, lusts for money and power were at the root of what went wrong in the church. In the first story, Ananias and Sapphira wanted the recognition a large gift often produces, and they were willing to lie to get it. In the second, Simon wanted spiritual influence and thought it could be bought with money. Power and money are still at the root of many problems which must be confronted by and among church leaders. Many moral failures, although expressed as sexual sins, are rooted in the quest for power or abuse of power in a trust-based relationship. Sex, money, and power are the unholy trinity of leadership failure.

Other books outline how to lead a healthy church discipline process or how to manage organizational supervisory procedures. That's beyond the scope of what we can do here. The more pressing issue for you is personal. How do you handle the responsibility of confronting sin in your church, ministry organization, or by another leader? Learning to do this is one of the hardest skills of Christian leadership. Here are some principles to help you do it.

First, get over your idealized view of Christian behavior. Don't be jaded but be realistic about your expectations. All Christians, including other leaders, are still sinners, and some will occasionally act out in the worst way. Accept this fact: Sooner or later you will face a situation that requires intervention. It's going to happen, so prepare for it long before the situation arises. Prepare spiritually but also practically. Have a game plan with procedures in place to handle problems before they come up.

Second, accept the complexity and messiness of situations requiring intervention. Affairs have perpetrators and victims and cause all kinds of collateral damage. Thieves are often manipulators who try to make you think you owed them the money. People who play power games are skillful and deceptive. Sorting out who has done what, who is at fault, who deserves discipline, and what those consequences will be is very difficult. Part of the struggle is accepting mixed outcomes. "Happily ever after" with all parties restored seldom happens. Sin is just too nasty to always be resolved cleanly.

Third, expect some Christians to resent you for taking a stand against sin. Some will claim you aren't being redemptive. Others will accuse you of being judgmental and warn you, "Judge not, lest you be judged." Some will takes sides because they are friends with the people involved. They will amaze you by how much they are willing to overlook, defending people they care for. This only intensifies when family members are involved. Beware of friendly fire when you take up the battle against sin.

Fourth, be wise about what you confront and how you confront it. Every Christian sins; no one is perfect. Not every sinful act has to be confronted in a big way. Sometimes a quiet corrective is all that's needed. Sin must be confronted among members or employees, however, when it compromises the integrity of a church or ministry organization. Among leaders, sin must be confronted when behavior violates trust—moral, ethical, or legal. Egregious behavior must be handled appropriately, directly, and sometimes publicly.

Finally, get outside counsel to help you through these situations. Even as a maturing spiritual leader, you are still susceptible to becoming emotionally entangled. When your friends, family, staff associates, or church members are involved, your judgment can become distorted. Your anger or fear can control you, clouding your judgment. You might respond too softly, overlooking real problems. You might slip into revenge mode, trying to punish or get even rather than seeking repentance and restoration. A pastoral friend or leadership peer in another organization can help you think through your options and actions. Denominational leaders, board members, legal advisors, professional consultants, or other trusted statesmen may need to be brought in when a situation is particularly problematic. Get the help you need to maintain your objectivity and equilibrium. Don't let pride or embarrassment keep you from getting others involved as needed.

Confronting sin is an ugly aspect of Christian leadership, but it must be done. It's an inevitable part of our responsibility to uphold appropriate standards among believers and, more specifically, among leaders. Integrity is a mandate, not an option. Do your part as the leader God has called you to be.

QUESTIONS FOR REFLECTION

1. When have you confronted sin in your church or organization? How did it go? What will you do differently next time?
2. What are your biggest challenges to confronting sin appropriately?
3. Which of the suggestions above is most helpful in strengthening you for this responsibility?
4. Which leadership lessons prepare you to confront sin?

Priority 8

EMBRACE NEW PARADIGMS

Acts 8:14–17

 Leaders live in the present, but with one eye fixed on the horizon. Part of your role is anticipating the future. No one can predict the future, but you must foresee coming trends and lead accordingly. One aspect of doing this is recognizing paradigm shifts—as opposed to fads—as genuine breakthroughs, inaugurating a new era. These can be local changes like shifting demographics in a church's ministry setting, or they can be global, like the availability of the Internet worldwide. Leaders observe paradigm shifts and lead accordingly. When God is moving in a new way, it's important to get in step and move forward with him. This isn't always easy. People have a hard time with change. Leaders have to lead—taking people forward when they may be afraid, reluctant, or even recalcitrant.

Peter had to make a decision about some startling events in Samaria. People there were claiming faith in Jesus. Was this a paradigm change or just a troublesome anomaly? Even though Jesus had said the gospel was for everyone and proved it clearly at Pentecost, the early church struggled with the concept. The Christian faith remained closely connected to the Jewish community and centered in Jerusalem. This pattern continued for several years. Eventually, persecution scattered the church. Philip, an early

Christian evangelist, made his way to Samaria and started leading people to faith in Jesus. When the Jerusalem church heard that people in Samaria were following Jesus, they sent Peter and John to check it out.

Who were the Samaritans, and why was it such a breakthrough for them to receive the gospel? The Jews hated the Samaritans; they were a mixed race, a conglomeration of various ethnicities intermarried with Jews over several generations. Jews avoided traveling through Samaria, shunned any contact with Samaritans, and considered them inferior. Samaritans maintained their own temple and were reciprocal in their antagonistic feelings toward the Jews. Jesus confounded this separation during his ministry by deliberately traveling through Samaria, healing a Samaritan leper, praising a Samaritan for his compassion, and asking a Samaritan woman for a drink. Nevertheless, the Jerusalem church perpetuated the Jewish prejudice toward Samaritans. When the gospel reached Samaria, it was controversial. Peter and John were dispatched as inquisitors, not encouragers. They were sent to evaluate this nascent movement and take appropriate action. Many probably hoped they would stamp out the heresy and keep the Jewish-Christian church pure. They were about to be surprised.

Peter arrived in Samaria, surveyed the situation, and affirmed the legitimacy of Samaritan conversion. Rather than limit or stop the movement, he discerned that something was missing—the filling of the Holy Spirit. The Samaritans had confessed their faith in Jesus and been baptized, but they hadn't received the Spirit. Perhaps the Spirit's advent was delayed for just this purpose—so Peter, the preacher of Pentecost, could also be part of the Spirit's inauguration of this new paradigm—the Samaritan conversion. Peter's presence brought credibility to the experience, not only for the Samaritans but also for the Jerusalem church which would soon hear what had happened. Peter's laying hands on the Samaritans not only facilitated Spirit-filling, but communicated his affirmation of the new paradigm that was dawning.

Anticipating the future is more than making educated guesses. You can improve your ability to discern future trends by several means. Start by taking seriously what God says about future events. Peter did. He heard Jesus say the gospel was for the whole world. He watched Jesus model that principle in the way he welcomed all kinds of people. He experienced Pentecost, the embodiment of God's plan to include all nations in his kingdom. Peter connected Old Testament prophecy to these events in his early sermons, thus underscoring his insight into God's long-standing intent to include all people in his plans. Peter models listening to what God says about the future and leading accordingly.

God has spoken about coming events, and it's not a pretty picture. The Bible describes the future this way: Sin will become more prevalent, wars will increase, human suffering will spread, and national economies will falter. Satan's influence will steadily rise, and righteousness will gradually wane. Even casual Bible readers recognize the future is bleak for those outside a relationship with God.

While those global predictions are clear, there's also prophecy in the Bible about the church. In contrast to a disintegrating world condition, the church will remain strong. It will be purified by trials and become an oasis of sanity for all who turn to Jesus. If you think the world is going to get better and better, your hope is misplaced. Jesus is the Hope of the world, despite how bad things will get, and his church will persevere to the end. Ultimately, the best day is yet to come—the day when Jesus returns. That's a future you can count on, and lead your ministry accordingly.

Another aspect of anticipating the future is watching for new ways and places that God is at work and joining him there. The gospel is surging in many places in the world. People are coming to Jesus in large numbers. Wise mission leaders are pouring additional resources, both human and financial, into those regions—striking while the iron is hot. As a leader, look for methods or programs God is blessing in other places and incorporate them into your work. Watch particularly for God at work "on the edges." Organizational analysts have discovered that innovation seldom comes from within a bureaucracy. It usually comes from the edges of organizational life or from completely outside the establishment. The application for churches and ministries is this: look to the edges, the places where there is less structure and more freedom to experiment. That's often the place God works to reveal new methodology.

You can also discern the future by paying attention to cultural trends and being an early adopter in your ministry setting. If you're reading this book in printed form, you're in a diminishing group. A growing number of people primarily read e-books. As a seminary leader, watching this trend has important applications for the future of libraries. What will a high-quality seminary library be like in 2030? The growing dominance of electronic media and new modes of information storage means it will be quite different than the ivy-covered retreat of past generations. That's just one example of future cultural trends impacting ministry planning.

What are the coming trends in interpersonal communication, sharing information, gathering resources, connecting people globally, and international travel? As you discover these answers, make application of these insights to your ministry setting. What are the future trends in spiritual belief and religious practice? While you may not accommodate or incorporate all these trends, you should be developing future strategies to engage people about the gospel in the context of those future realities.

Finally, you can anticipate the future by listening to professional futurists. Some are quacks who try to convince you they can predict the future. They can't. Legitimate futurists are experts at data mining and discovering the demographic, social, political, and economic trends that are determining the future of our world. For example, the birth rate right now is historically low in North America. Futurists can forecast the implications of that data on youth ministry in the next decade. Birth rate will also impact college enrollment in the decade after that. You can't expect burgeoning growth that depends on people who were never born. Paying attention to researchers who gather data revealing future trends is an important way to read the signs of the times.

Peter understood times were changing when he arrived in Samaria. While he may have lacked some of the resources just described, he had the spiritual insight to recognize the future as God revealed it to him. In short, he recognized that God was doing something new and joined him in the process. Ask God to give you the same insight. Ask him to help you live in the future, anticipating how he is working and will work. Keep your church or ministry on the cutting edge. While this may be painful for those around you resisting the change, leaders don't settle for the status quo. They embrace new paradigms as they emerge in God's ever-changing kingdom.

QUESTIONS FOR REFLECTION

1. Why is it important to recognize new paradigms and join them?
2. What is one way your church or ministry needs to change to move toward the future?
3. Which of the suggestions above is most helpful for anticipating the future? How will you implement it?
4. Which leadership lessons prepare you to embrace new paradigms?

Priority 9

LEADERS CHANGE THEIR MINDS

Acts 9:43–10:48

 Leaders have strong opinions. We study long and hard before we make up our minds, then we hold to our positions. I sometimes joke, "I may be wrong, but I'm never in doubt." Leaders hold convictions. We don't adopt every new idea that comes along. We cherish timeless truth and implement proven strategies. We aren't swayed by every wind of doctrine or Web-driven fad. Despite how firmly we hold our convictions, we are also learners—meaning we are open to new ideas (like the paradigm shifts described in the last chapter). When we discover new insights, we are humble enough to change our minds. When we are wrong, we admit it and move forward.

Peter's travels took him to Joppa, where he stayed in the home of Simon the tanner, foreshadowing significant coming events. Peter's willingness to stay with a person who practiced an unclean occupation indicated his openness to relate to people individually, despite his Jewish law and tradition. Another man, Cornelius, lived in Caesarea about a day's walk away. He was a Roman centurion and a devout God-fearer. One afternoon, Cornelius had a vision of an angel who told him to send to Joppa for a man named Peter. He promptly dispatched two servants and a soldier to retrieve him.

The next day about noon, while Peter was hungry for lunch, he also had a vision. He saw a large sheet descending from heaven filled with all kinds of animals. A voice told him to kill something and eat. Peter reverted to an old pattern. "No, Lord!" he replied. His reason: "I have never eaten anything common and ritually unclean!" The voice spoke again, "What God has made clean, you must not call common." The sequence was repeated three times, and then the sheet disappeared into heaven. Three times—perhaps reminding Peter of his previous threefold experiences with the Lord.

Peter was perplexed and wondering what the vision meant, when three messengers (three again) arrived at Simon's house looking for him. The Spirit prompted Peter to receive the men, hear their message from Cornelius, and go with them to Caesarea. When they arrived, Cornelius assembled his family and friends to hear Peter speak.

Peter told them it was forbidden for a Jewish man to visit a foreigner's home but that God had changed his mind. "God has shown me," Peter said, "that I must not call any person common or unclean." Then he asked Cornelius why he had sent for him. Cornelius recounted his vision and the steps he had taken to follow the instructions he'd received, culminating in a request for Peter to teach them whatever God had revealed to him.

Peter grasped the full meaning of the events of the past three (three again) days. He said, "Now I really understand that God doesn't show favoritism. . . . He is Lord of all." Peter then preached a gospel message, but before he could finish, the Holy Spirit intervened. The Gentiles gathered in Cornelius' home began speaking in tongues and praising God. Commentators debate if this was languages like Pentecost or ecstatic utterances. Whatever was verbalized, Peter recognized it as legitimizing their conversion, and he baptized all who believed in Jesus.

Peter changed his mind about the most crucial issue facing the early church—the nature of the gospel. It wasn't only for Jews and Samaritans (partial Jews). It was also for Gentiles (non-Jews). The people Jews had shunned for centuries, God was including as full participants in his kingdom. While this seems common today, it was an incredibly dramatic breakthrough in its time. The gospel, promised to everyone by Jesus, really was for everyone—even the cursed Gentiles. God moved Peter through an elaborate three-day process, with a threefold vision, in response to three messengers to establish the gospel among the Gentiles. Peter, the most significant leader in the early church, had changed his mind. The gospel was now for everyone and would explode across the Mediterranean world very soon through the church at Antioch (Acts 11:19–26).

Peter changed his mind about the most important doctrinal issue in church history. He would follow through on his new understanding of the gospel at the Jerusalem Council (Acts 15). At that watershed event, he sided with the delegation from Antioch, the first Gentile church. He also rejected the Judaizers' insistence that conversion could only follow circumcision—the Gentile must become a Jew first, then a Christian. Peter's influence helped win the day for salvation by grace through faith, apart from any human agency or activity. When Peter changed his mind about the scope of the gospel's reach, he stayed with his new conviction, even when it created tension with people who held a position he formerly supported. He disagreed with the leaders in Jerusalem, his home church, to preserve the universal availability of the gospel.

Leaders change their minds. They learn new things and grow. That's why you are reading this book. You want to learn new insights and be more effective at what you do. When you discover you are wrong about something, you change your mind. But with all the new information generated daily and all the different biblical interpretations being proposed, how do you know when to change your mind?

The most obvious answer is when God teaches you something new. God speaks primarily through the Bible and never in contradiction of the Bible. Ignoring that reality is how cults get started and how some leaders confuse people with "special" or "private" interpretations. These cautions should not, however, keep you from pursuing and expecting new insights from studying God's Word.

The Bible is an amazing book. A child can understand it the first time they read it, and a scholar can't grasp its full meaning with a lifetime of study. No matter how much you know about the Bible, there's always more to learn. As you change and your ministry setting changes, your learning readiness for new insights also changes. As you learn more sophisticated ways to study the Bible, you learn deeper insights. Being able to study the Bible in its original languages, for example, opens up a treasure trove of additional insights.

Improving your study skills, while simultaneously moving through the leadership seasons, produces a synergistic progression, interweaving biblical truth with life and ministry needs. This produces new insights at just the right time to keep you growing and developing as a leader. Only God can do this! He has a magnificent capacity to shape you continually throughout your lifetime. God will change your thinking in important ways at crucial times.

You should also change your mind when you learn new, non-contradictory, extra-biblical information. For me, learning accounting principles changed my thinking about corporate financial management. Understanding employment law made me a better personnel administrator. Discovering my preferred learning style, my personality profile, my way of expressing and receiving love, and how my upbringing shaped my psyche changed me in many ways. Formal education, continuing education, and personal growth are important for leaders. As you learn new information, change your mind, and change your practices, you become a different and better leader.

You should also change your mind when you're wrong. If "I love you" are the three most powerful words in a romantic relationship, then "I was wrong" may be the three most important words in a leadership relationship. Some leaders simply can't admit fault. When pressed, one leader told me he could not remember one—not even one—significant leadership mistake he had ever made. He wrongly assumed that showing weakness, even in a private conversation, would diminish his leadership stature in the eyes of his followers.

Some leaders believe that admitting fault, expressing uncertainty, or changing their mind lowers their esteem among their followers. The opposite is true. Pride in their pseudo perfection masks their insecurity—but only for the leader who thinks he's fooling everyone. Followers see through the charade and long for honesty. Admitting doubt or uncertainly establishes humanity and creates authenticity in leadership relationships. Beyond that, owning up when you have been wrong strengthens your relationships with followers. It demonstrates humility and invites others to help you think more clearly or find new solutions.

When you are wrong, admit it. When you need to change your mind, do it. Learn to work through both processes faster. When the horse dies, dismount! Change your thinking, chart a new course, and lead on.

QUESTIONS FOR REFLECTION

1. What is a significant way you have changed your mind about ministry leadership? Was it a tough process? Why or why not?
2. Do you regularly learn new insights from the Bible? If not, why not?
3. Is it hard for you to admit you are wrong? Why or why not?
4. Which leadership lessons prepare you to change your mind?

DEFEND THE FAITH

Acts 11:1–18; 15:6–11

 Leaders change their minds—only, sometimes they don't. They stand strong in the face of opposition, even opposition from other Christians trying to dissuade them from their convictions. Leaders defend the core doctrines of the Christian faith without compromise, often with devastating personal consequences. Pastors are terminated, professors fired, churches split, denominations come unraveled, and sadly, martyrs die rather than deny the faith. Leaders defend the faith.

Peter changed his mind about the nature of the gospel. He was convinced of his new position by the Samaritan Pentecost, his vision in Joppa, and the experiences at Cornelius' house. The gospel was for everyone, even the formerly hated Gentiles. Once he settled this matter, nothing moved him from his newfound position, even though he faced formidable opposition. He had to face down former colleagues and friends in his home church in Jerusalem.

It didn't take long for word of what had happened with Peter to spread through the Jewish community. When Peter arrived back in Jerusalem, the church's leaders were waiting for him. Those who insisted circumcision was a precursor to or a part of salvation weren't backing down from their position. They argued with Peter and accused him of visiting uncircumcised men and eating with them.

While it sounds ridiculous to modern ears, try to place yourself in the moment. For centuries, Jews had practiced various laws and traditions to keep themselves separate from Gentiles. Early believers probably thought they had come a long way in overcoming their prejudice by allowing Gentiles to become Christians, as long as they became Jews first (symbolized by circumcision). Now Peter was going a step farther. He concluded that Gentiles could become Christians by grace through faith, becoming full heirs of God's promises and participants in his kingdom. Gentile believers, just like Jewish believers, were children of God. Scandalous indeed!

Peter told the story of what happened with Cornelius' family and friends, beginning with his vision in Joppa and concluding with the advent of the Spirit among them. When he finished, the Jerusalem leaders were silent for a while—perhaps shocked, or maybe just mulling over what they had heard. Then they glorified God with this conclusion: "So God has granted repentance resulting in life even to the Gentiles!" Happy ending— if only it had been the end. The problem would fester as more and more Gentiles believed in Jesus.

When the gospel arrived in Antioch, it found its first mass reception among Gentiles. Large numbers of Gentiles came to faith in Jesus without being circumcised. Barnabas was dispatched from Jerusalem to check out the new movement. He affirmed what he discovered and fetched Paul from Tarsus to launch a teaching ministry stabilizing the new church. Tension mounted between Antioch and Jerusalem—so intense that a delegation had to be sent from Antioch to Jerusalem to work out the problem. Once for all, the church had to decide the nature of the gospel.

When the Antioch delegation arrived in Jerusalem, Peter was among the leaders who welcomed them. When the formal meetings began, the discussion was barely civil—an argument that truly reached "biblical proportions." Paul and Barnabas, leaders from Antioch, debated the Jerusalem leaders who held the position, "It is necessary to circumcise them [Gentiles] and to command them to keep the law of Moses!"

Peter was present for the debate. He listened to all sides, perhaps participating or just taking it all in. The Bible doesn't say how long the meeting lasted. It could even have been several meetings over several days.

While the duration isn't clear from Scripture, the intensity certainly is. The group engaged in "much debate." You can only imagine what this must have been like, given the importance of the doctrine, the history behind the issues, the prejudice being confronted, and the ego strength of these giants of Christian leadership. It was like a spiritual cage match.

After a while, Peter stood up (we have encountered that phrase before) and offered his observation and conclusion. He reminded them of his role in early Gentile conversions and sided with those who were supportive of all Gentiles coming to faith in Jesus without circumcision or fulfillment of any other law. He concluded: "On the contrary, we believe we are saved through the grace of the Lord Jesus in the same way they are." This calmed the crowd, which fell silent. Paul and Barnabas then shared their experiences among the Gentiles. James, a Jerusalem leader, proposed the solution finally adopted: The gospel was for everyone and salvation was by grace through faith in Jesus. Nothing more, nothing less.

Leaders, when they are absolutely convinced, stand up for doctrinal convictions. The pertinent question, though, is which doctrines are truly convictions and require an absolute commitment to uphold? To help sort this out, consider this schematic (borrowed from my book, *The Case for Antioch*) to help you answer the question. There are three levels of Christian belief—convictions, commitments, and preferences.

The most important doctrines are "convictions." These doctrines define the Christian faith. They are nonnegotiable. When a person denies one of these, they deny the faith. When a Christian church, denomination, or school rejects one of these, they are no longer, by definition, a Christian entity. Doctrines of God, salvation, and Scripture fall into this category but are not an exhaustive list. Convictions are the "here I stand" issues demarcating the Christian faith.

How do you know if something belongs in this category? Without being flippant, these are doctrines worth dying for. Most believers in Western churches don't face this reality, but believers around the world do. Some truth is worth dying for . . . and some isn't. Knowing the difference is vital to successfully defending the faith while avoiding pointless arguments over lesser issues.

The second level of doctrinal positions is called "commitments." These commitments are very important beliefs that define vital issues. While they aren't give-your-life issues, it's still important to have genuine commitments to positions, perspectives, and practices represented by these doctrines. Shared commitments are the basis for local church fellowship. For example, while various models of church government are permissible, no church will survive very long if its members are in continual disagreement about how to make decisions. A congregation needs a shared set of commitments about church order so decisions can be made and progress achieved.

Similarly, issues like eschatological positions, charismatic/noncharismatic practices, and observances of church ordinances fall into this category. One example of such alignments for groups of churches is denominationalism. Christians form churches defined by these issues, and those churches form denominations to work together with minimal distraction. When churches share the same convictions (making them Christian churches) and generally share the same commitments (defined by doctrinal positions on these second-tier issues), they are able to work together effectively.

Finally, the third level of doctrinal position is called "preference." These are positions that reflect changing tastes, regional or national biases, cultural factors, political persuasions, and generational differences. Some might argue these aren't doctrinal issues at all, but they are because Christians often claim biblical support for their positions. For most Christians, issues like educational strategies (home school, Christian school, public school), missionary methods (independent, societal, associational), and preaching style (topical, expository) fall into this category. We have preferences, but we recognize these issues don't define Christianity nor is agreement necessary for local church or denominational effectiveness. There is wide latitude among most believers, as there should be, on these issues. We may or may not work closely together with believers or churches who don't share our preferences, but nonetheless, we appreciate their contribution to kingdom work.

Your fundamental challenge is to identify your convictions and hold to them without compromise while at the same time demonstrating patience and grace with other believers who have differing commitments and preferences. Leaders stand strong on what matters and cooperate deferentially on lesser issues with those who agree with them on core convictions. Leaders defend the faith by standing for doctrinal convictions that define the faith. On other matters, we strive for common ground and mutual respect as we work together.

QUESTIONS FOR REFLECTION

1. Have you had to take a stand on a doctrinal conviction? What happened? In hindsight, would you do anything differently?
2. Do you agree with the convictions, commitments, and preferences model? Why or why not?
3. What is a core doctrinal issue in your ministry setting that requires taking a stand? How will you do it?
4. Which leadership lessons prepare you to defend the faith?

Priority 11

LEADERS REST IN GOD'S PROTECTION

Acts 12:1–19

Leaders take risks and need protection. Fortunately, God has your back. Christian leaders rest in God's protection. Peter discovered this during intense persecution by Herod, a violent ruler who opposed the church.

Herod's soldiers attacked the church and killed James, John's brother, one of the original Twelve—taking his life "with the sword." This pleased the Jews and increased Herod's popularity. He then arrested Peter, had him imprisoned, and prepared to kill him to gain even more favor with the Jewish community. Peter was heavily guarded, with four squads of four soldiers each rotating the duty. He was also bound with two chains, possibly connected to his captors as an added means of security.

Peter was sleeping between two guards on the night before his planned execution, when an angel awakened him. The angel told him to get up, get dressed, and follow him. Peter's chains fell off, and he was soon in the street, trailing the angel leading him to safety. They passed two guard posts before arriving at an iron gate, which opened by itself. Once through the gate and on a familiar street, the angel left Peter who concluded, "The Lord has sent His angel and rescued me."

Peter then went to a house owned by a prominent woman, which was a common gathering place for worship. Many Christians were having a prayer meeting—most likely for Peter's deliverance. Peter banged on the door, and a servant girl named Rhoda answered. She recognized Peter's voice and ran to tell the others he was at the gate—while, in another humorous moment in Scripture, she left Peter cooling his heels in the street. "You're crazy," was the response of the gathered believers. After all, they were busy praying for imprisoned Peter's release—he couldn't be at the gate. But he was! When they finally let him in, he told them the miraculous story of the angelic intervention. He told them to pass the word of his release along to the other church leaders and then he left, moving to a safer place to hide from a potential search party. At daybreak, Herod interrogated the guards who had lost Peter. He then ordered their execution and left for Caesarea, leaving Peter free to continue leading the church.

God protects leaders. He delivers them from trouble, protects them when they get in trouble, and guides them through trouble. God also prevents some problems from ever happening, hence we don't always recognize his protection. He protects us when we are doing his work, even when it involves real risk. My friend Mike's story is an inspiring example:

My family was living in Germany, and we were members of the International Baptist Church in Stuttgart. Several former residents of Eastern-bloc countries also attended the church. Eventually, many of their countries, including Romania, opened their borders. In response, our church sent teams into formerly closed communist countries. We took food, clothes, and other relief goods, but also Bibles in the Hungarian and Romanian languages. We drove these supplies into Romania in two-man teams.

Tensions remained high. The border crossings were stressful. Travel was difficult. The churches we visited welcomed us and celebrated their newfound freedoms. All went smoothly until we drove into what we thought was a small village. The hand-drawn map the local church had mailed us depicted only six streets, so we thought we could easily find the Baptist church. Imagine our shock when we arrived in a large city, not a village. The map was useless. We had no information but the name of the street and the name of the church. We were lost.

We began asking pedestrians for directions. We spoke only English and German, not Romanian or Hungarian. People seemed sympathetic but responded with confused shrugs. After the third or fourth attempt to get directions, we were surprised by a small, red Trabant that pulled in front of our car. Its horn honked. An arm stuck out of the driver's window and waved for us to follow. With no other viable options, we decided we would. Several miles and turns later, the Trabant stopped. We were on an isolated dirt road. We knew several vehicles hauling trailers of relief goods had been hijacked. Suddenly, following this strange car didn't seem like it had been such a good decision.

Just as we were wondering what to do next, the driver honked his horn again, stuck his arm out the window and pointed over the roof of his car. We looked past a wall and saw the top of a building with the name of the church painted on its side. The driver honked again, waved good-bye, and drove away.

Later, we asked the pastor whom he had sent for us. "No one," he replied, "we received a letter telling us you were coming, but it didn't say when you would arrive." "Who in your congregation drives a red Trabant," we asked. "No one," he replied. "I've never even seen a red Trabant. They are normally black."

No one in the church had ever seen this car. We never found the driver. We never saw anything but his arm. He didn't talk to us before leading us to the church. The people we spoke to on the street gave no indication they understood what we needed, so we don't believe anyone summoned the driver. He never asked for anything, and every other stranger who assisted us always did.

I don't know who our guide was or how he knew our destination. All I know is he was there when we needed help. Ever since that day, in moments of confusion and need, I find myself anticipating God's provision. He hasn't sent any more red Trabants, but through his Word and his people he has never failed to provide guidance, and that knowledge inspires comfort and confidence.

Does angelic intervention still happen in our world? Yes. While it's difficult to prove, stories like Mike's indicate some type of supernatural intervention. Did an angel drive the car? Possibly. In any case, by some inexplicable means, God protected a leader doing his work in a dangerous location.

While we celebrate God's protection, an important question is raised by another aspect of Peter's story. God sent an angel to deliver Peter from prison and guide him to freedom. If God protects leaders, why was Peter arrested in the first place? Why not just send an angel to strike down the captors, publicly and powerfully protecting this church leader? Beyond that, why was Peter's life ultimately spared while James was killed? If God protects leaders, what about James? Was he less valuable to the church, his family, or God's plans? Why did God deliver one and allow the other to die?

The ultimate answers are incomprehensible, shrouded in the mystery of God's plans and purposes, not only for individuals, but for the global advance of his kingdom. This much is certain from Peter's story: God protects leaders until they have fulfilled his purposes for them. God will sustain your life until he has used you to do all he has planned for you, until your impact is fully exhausted, and until his purpose through you is accomplished. James died sooner than Peter. Only God knows the reasons one leader was martyred while the other was delivered by an angel—both in the providence of God.

You can have confidence in God's sustaining power. You will live the length of time he intends. He will accomplish through you every God-assigned leadership task before your life ends. God will use you for his glory—in life and in death—and he gets to decide the duration of your service.

My friend Casey was a significant leader. He died far too young, when it seemed there was so much more he could have done. His death left a huge hole in our hearts. Other men—child abusers, porn peddlers, and human traffickers continue to live. Why this injustice? I don't know why God allows some to live and others to die. God's ways are far beyond our limited understanding of these matters.

God's protection gives you confidence. Your life is in his hands. He will sustain you to your maximum usefulness. You won't die one day sooner than he has planned, or one day later. You can lead without fear, taking

risks to advance God's kingdom, trusting the length of your life to God—
the only Person who has power over life and death.

Questions for Reflection

1. Are you hampered by fears that limit your leadership effectiveness? How does Peter's example help you to confront those fears?
2. Has God ever protected you in an unusual way? How does this
   encourage you about the future?
3. Do you believe God will sustain your life as long as he intends? If
   so, how does this increase your confidence?
4. Which leadership lessons prepare you to rest in God's protection?

Priority 12

WORK WITH OTHER LEADERS

Galatians 1:18; 2:6–10; 1 Corinthians 1:12; 3:22; 9:5

 Everyone loves a hero. Heroic portrayals tell dramatic stories of leaders standing alone against all odds, taking on forces of evil and coming out victorious despite formidable foes. Sounds exciting, but that's seldom how effective leadership really works. Most leadership challenges aren't life-or-death struggles, just complex problems demanding creative, insightful solutions. These are best discovered when leaders work with others—both their followers and often with other leaders. Effective leaders work with others to accomplish more than they can do on their own.

Peter is such a towering figure, it's easy to overlook how he partnered with other leaders to advance God's kingdom. One particular friendship/ partnership is particularly interesting. After Paul became a Christian and spent three years in Damascus, he presented himself to the Jerusalem church. Peter welcomed him, invited him to his home, and spent about two weeks with him. Like when Churchill met Roosevelt to plan the details about fighting World War II, these titanic church leaders held a private meeting that changed the world. Imagine their conversations as they talked theology, missiology, and ministry philosophy. Consider what might have been said about church growth, responding to persecution, and expanding the reach of the gospel.

Peter's inviting Paul into his home was like Billy Graham welcoming a recently converted radical imam into his. Until his conversion, Paul was a religious terrorist—he killed Christians and created chaos in the church. Paul's return to Jerusalem, from where he had been dispatched on his Sanhedrin-authorized murder mission, was dramatic and controversial. Peter took a great risk welcoming Paul, not only as a friend but also into church leadership. People haven't changed in two thousand years. Think about the gossip that must have flown around Jerusalem about Peter's behavior. Nevertheless, Peter recognized the legitimacy of Paul's conversion and his potential as a missionary and church leader. Peter associated himself with Paul, validated his leadership potential, and helped launch him into his new role.

According to Paul's account, the meeting with Peter resulted in a division of labor as both men continued to lead kingdom advance. Paul was charged to go aggressively to the Gentiles, communicating the gospel and starting churches among them. Peter, on the other hand, would continue his primary ministry among Jews. Peter had been instrumental in authenticating Gentile evangelism and church-planting, no doubt smoothing the way for the Jerusalem church to embrace the movement. Paul, however, would be the primary leader in expanding the gospel to all people. This was a mutual decision, endorsed by other key leaders, and sealed with the right hand of fellowship. Later, when Paul led the delegation to Jerusalem to resolve the issue of Gentile-inclusion once for all, Peter made the deciding speech finalizing the matter. Their relationship started with two weeks spent together early in Paul's leadership career and culminated in standing together to determine the doctrine of salvation by grace through faith for everyone, for all time. These two spiritual giants built a friendship enabling them to stand together when it mattered most.

Paul later wrote positively about Peter. He cautioned believers about forming personality cults around prominent leaders like Peter or anyone else, including himself. He used Peter's marriage as an example of appropriate domestic relations among Christian leaders. He also referred to Peter's practice of receiving financial support from other believers as validating that model for missionary support. Peter reciprocated by equating Paul's writings with Scripture, an early recognition of the unique place his letters to the churches would have in shaping the church for centuries to come. Clearly, these two men respected each other, learned from one another, and worked together to advance God's kingdom.

Leaders work with other leaders. A mark of maturity is your willingness to attract, work with, and learn from other leaders. The best leaders aren't loners living in an egotistical delusion that they can do it all on their own. Effective leaders recognize the value of interacting with and partnering with other dynamic leaders. Doing this requires humility and admitting you don't know it all. It also requires deference—allowing others to lead when their intellectual or experiential capacities exceed yours. Developing these character qualities is essential for attracting other leaders to your team. Practicing these qualities improves both your organizational performance and personal leadership stature. There are a variety of models for doing this today.

One way to work with other leaders is to add them to your team, intentionally and strategically filling in your leadership weaknesses. For most pastors, this means allowing laymen and women to use their gifts in partnership with yours. In my early pastoral ministry, I failed at this. I attended every committee meeting and met with every program director, making sure my opinion was heard and my directions followed. I overestimated my leadership abilities and feared losing control of decision-making. I was afraid of admitting weakness, which in my mind, diminished my leadership stature.

Through all this, my insecurities were revealed and my stature really diminished. Only when I became secure enough to share leadership with others did this change. To my surprise, adding people to my leadership circle elevated my leadership stature. When you add other leaders to your team, your followers will respect you more, not less. They already know your limitations. Admitting them and asking other people to fill in the gaps, thus creating a powerful leadership group (rather than the self-deluded superstar approach), gives your followers greater confidence in and appreciation for your leadership. It's counterintuitive but true. When you partner with other leaders, it increases your leadership stature. When you go it alone and refuse to admit weakness and learn from others, confidence in your leadership wanes.

In larger churches or ministry organizations, attracting other leaders means recruiting employees who offset your weaknesses. Some leaders hire clones—people who think and act just like them. That's a recipe for organizational disaster. Wise leaders attract other leaders who share their mission, but who bring contrasting perspectives and gifts to the team. Peter and Paul are an example of this kind of relationship. They shared one mission but were quite different in their approach to accomplishing it. They appreciated one another—they were even friends—but there was an underlying tension in their approaches to ministry (not always underlying, as you will see in the next chapter). Strong leaders, who are also wise leaders, choose other strong leaders to work with them. Doing this leads to tension and debate on important decisions. As long as everyone on the team is aligned on the mission and will unify around the final decision, spirited discussion about the best way to move forward is an asset. In my current high-performance leadership team, I find that our meetings aren't really going well until someone is pounding the table. I want a team filled with passionate leaders who challenge my ideas. "Yes men" are useless.

Another way leaders work with other leaders is by cooperating with those of other churches, denominations, or ministry organizations. Today, many churches and ministries have lost their narrow mission focus and think they can do just about anything. Good leaders keep their organization lashed to its mission and cooperate with other leaders and ministries that specialize in other specific endeavors. Not every church, for example, needs to have an adoption service or manage a church-planting infrastructure. Wise leaders find other specialized leaders and trust them as ministry partners.

Finally, good leaders work with other leaders by making friends with them. Loneliness is an occupational hazard of Christian leadership. Many leaders are too busy to make friends. While hyper productivity may produce short-term success, taking time to invest in relationships will sustain you for the long haul. It's good to have ministry peers who are also friends. When the pressure is on, those relationships form the backbone for a coalition to stand together in a crucial moment. Peter and Paul forged a relationship during two weeks together in Peter's home. Later, that relationship played a part in their standing together at the Jerusalem Council. It also gave them the relational base to withstand an ugly conflict (described in the next chapter) that could have shattered early church fellowship. You will benefit from friendships with other leaders. Take time to cultivate them as an investment in your future success.

QUESTIONS FOR REFLECTION

1. How can you attract other leaders to your team?
2. Do you recruit team members who are like you or do you recruit to your weaknesses? Why or why not?
3. Who are some other leaders you consider your friends? What can you do to strengthen those relationships?
4. Which leadership lessons prepare you to work with other leaders?

Priority 13

MAKE MISTAKES AND MOVE ON

Galatians 2:11–21

 As we've already explored, emerging leaders make mistakes—sometimes a lot of mistakes. They hope that by the time they reach the leading season, they will be more skilled and not make so many of them. Well, bad news. Veteran, experienced, fully committed Christian leaders still make mistakes. A lot of them. I wish that weren't true; my life would be so much simpler.

As we improve our skills, develop our character, and gain more experience, we usually make fewer mistakes. We may also learn to quickly recognize a bad decision and chart a corrective course. Effective leaders are more likely to get counsel from others—particularly on technical issues like legal matters. This more deliberate approach also cuts down on mistakes. Hopefully, we also develop greater sensitivity to God's direction along with "leadership radar"—a spiritual sense of when something is out of whack and caution is in order. Heeding those spiritual impulses helps eliminate mistakes. Despite all this, however, we still mess things up. It's inevitable. Our sin-tainted minds, not-yet-fully-sanctified egos, and limited intellectual capacities assure the obvious—mistakes still happen.

Peter made a colossal blunder which earned him the ire of Paul, along with a public confrontation about his duplicity. Given the pains God had taken to educate Peter on the inclusion of the Gentiles and Peter's staunch support of that position at the Jerusalem Council, it's almost inconceivable that his big mistake could be related to the Gentile issue. But it was. His public misstep threatened the fellowship of the church and swayed other leaders to follow his bad example.

Peter was in the habit of eating with Gentiles—scandalous behavior to Judaizers who maintained the conviction that God's true people must separate from uncircumcised "sinners." Table fellowship was a sign of full acceptance; sharing a meal was the height of Christian inclusion. Some men came from the Jerusalem church to visit Peter. They were of the circumcision party, meaning they required adherence to that custom for any man who wanted a true relationship with God. Trusting Jesus was fine, but only after circumcision was it supposedly effectual for salvation. Peter had once been part of that group, but he had changed his mind and now publically advocated a different position (described in previous chapters). When the Judaizers arrived, however, Peter stopped eating with the Gentiles. He influenced others to join him, including Barnabas, who had also been an early champion of Gentile conversion apart from circumcision.

When Paul wrote about this incident, he minced no words. He called Peter's actions "hypocrisy." Paul saw this as more than a fellowship issue or an accommodation to conscience. He was convinced Peter was "deviating from the truth of the gospel." The issue became public as Paul confronted Peter "in front of everyone"—meaning the full assembly; both Gentiles and Judaizers, along with Peter and Barnabas. Everyone was aware of Peter's mistake and Paul's response.

Imagine what that must have been like—Peter and Paul, the two heavyweights of the New Testament era, squaring off in a battle royal. In one corner, tall and weathered from a lifetime of fishing—the companion of Jesus, the rock of the church, the preacher of Pentecost—the apostle Peter. And in the other corner, stooped and worn from tentmaking—converted terrorist, writer extraordinaire, church-planting catalyst—the apostle Paul. When the bell rang on this conflict, the sound reverberated through the ages. This wasn't a backroom, off-the-record discussion. It was a public showdown. Peter had blown it and because of his leadership stature, the consequences were blunt, direct, and public.

Leaders make mistakes. No matter how hard you try, you will make mistakes. You will make some of them in public and will pay the price of public correction. It may not be as intense as what Paul inflicted on Peter, but having your shortcomings known in any way is painful. Leaders live out loud, on stage, and in front of our followers, so our mistakes are often well-publicized. That's one of the inherent risks we assume when we take on the mantle of leadership.

Since mistakes are inevitable, what should you do when you make one? Start by understanding there are two kinds of mistakes leaders make—poor decisions and sinful choices. The first is simply a decision that didn't work out quite right. You may have hired the wrong person, picked a bad youth camp, or bought an inadequate computer system. You did the best you could and got less than stellar results. A sinful choice, on the other hand, has ethical or moral dimensions. When your mistake is a sinful choice, you have dishonored God and usually wronged another person (or many people). Examples might include exploding in anger at a staff member, manipulating the outcome of a meeting, or lying to cover misspent resources. These are more than bad decisions, they are sinful choices.

The first step in handling either kind of mistake is to take full responsibility for what you have done. Avoid shuffling the blame to others. You picked the bad camp. It's not the fault of the person who recommended it to you. You blew up in a meeting. Blaming your bad temper on your daddy is unacceptable. Take responsibility for your bad decisions and sinful choices. Brand them with your initials. Own them. They belong to you.

The next step is admitting you were wrong. Say those horrible-tasting words, "I was wrong." Practice them so you can actually get them out in front of other people.

Once you've admitted you were wrong, the next steps vary depending on what kind of mistake you made. If your mistake was a bad decision, admit you were wrong and apologize for what you did. Remember, a good apology says, "I was wrong and I am sorry *for*. . . ." Avoid the pseudo apology of "I am sorry *if*. . . ." The key word in a genuine apology is *for*, not *if*.

If your mistake was a sinful choice, then admit you were wrong, apologize for your actions, and confess yours sin—to God and to everyone directly involved. Confessing sin can be very difficult for a leader. Keep these simple steps in mind.

First, confess sin without blaming other people. You sinned because of your choice, not because the church failed to properly monitor your actions. Your sins are your responsibility. Don't try to blame others.

Second, confess your sin in the scope in which it was committed. If you lost your temper in a deacons' meeting, go apologize to the deacons. If you yelled at your assistant, apologize to her.

Third, confess your sin as personally as possible. Much communication is nonverbal. When you apologize and confess sin in person, the recipient senses sincerity in your mannerisms and vocal tones. If you can't go in person, make a phone call. Stay away from e-mail—it's a very poor media for deeply personal messages.

When you admit a mistake (whether bad decision or sinful choice), the next step is to accept your consequences. Some leaders blow the process at this point. They resist consequences and expect people to forgive and forget their mistakes. If you employed several people who haven't panned out, you need coaching on your hiring practices. If you overspent your budget, you need guidance on money management. When your mistakes earn consequences, accept them graciously and learn from them. Like Peter, since you lead in public, your mistakes may be well known and so may the consequences. That's part of being a leader. As you learn from and manage your consequences, your leadership freedoms will most likely be restored in due time.

Finally, when you make a mistake and handle it properly through the process just described, move on. Don't berate yourself over forgiven issues. Don't proudly claim, "God has forgiven me, but I just can't forgive myself." Are your standards higher than those of the Sovereign of the Universe? Quit arrogantly using that bogus claim for self-flagellation. When you admit a mistake and handle it properly, it's over. Put the consequences in perspective, refocus on your leadership responsibilities, and get moving. You have important work to do, other matters need your attention, and you probably have more mistakes to make. So get on with it. You're a leader and you can't afford to wallow in the past—particularly past mistakes.

One final encouragement—most mistakes are not fatal to your ministry. You will survive. While you may encounter a few hypercritical, difficult people, most of your followers want you to succeed and will tolerate your mistakes when you deal with them properly. Handle your mistakes with integrity, and your leadership will be sustained and strengthened. Peter continued as a leader—ultimately writing his legacy letters to which we now turn our attention. Leaders who make mistakes and handle them appropriately are still useful to God.

QUESTIONS FOR REFLECTION

1. What's an example of a bad leadership decision you have made? A sinful choice?
2. Did you handle these mistakes according to the process outlined in this chapter? If not, how could you have handled them better?
3. Why is it hard for you to move on from a leadership mistake? How will you improve this discipline?
4. Which leadership lessons prepare you for dealing with your mistakes?

Part Three

CONVICTIONS OF
MATURING LEADERS

Introduction

Just as learning gives way to leading, time and experience ultimately give way to the final season of leadership, when maturing leaders ultimately enter their final leadership season—leaving their legacy. During this phase, you become more concerned with what you are leaving behind than building something new. Your focus shifts to the next generation, to facilitating their success rather than your own. Peter lived to and through this season, leaving a written legacy for his followers and for all believers for all time. His written legacy is part of Scripture, the books known as 1 and 2 Peter. Your contribution won't reach that level, but it's significant, nonetheless. All leaders have influence, and your influence can be projected into the future, just like Peter's was, long after you are gone.

Leaving a legacy begs the question, "What is a legacy?" Some people consider their legacy their record of achievements. Football coaches focus on wins and losses; school teachers, on their graduates; and soldiers, their years of service. Others leave their legacy as a monument—a statue on a campus, a building with their name on it, or a plaque hanging on a wall. People also think of legacy as money they've accumulated and left behind—either as a bequest or perhaps creating a charitable foundation benefiting others. These can all be valid markers of a life well lived. There's nothing necessarily wrong with recording a lifetime of achievements, creating a tangible remembrance, or leaving behind a lot of money. All of these accomplishments can inspire and bless others.

None of these, however, describe the kind of living legacy Peter left us. They all have one negative in common—they lack permanence. Records are broken, monuments crumble, and money gets spent or lost. A lasting legacy is a living legacy. Peter models a threefold living legacy in his two short letters. You leave your best legacy when you follow his model.

Your living legacy is *the wisdom you have gained, the people you have influenced, and the convictions you model which inspire a subsequent generation.* When you leave a living legacy, you've invested the wisdom you've learned over your lifetime into your followers. You have learned much about life and leadership through Scripture, experience, and reflective discernment. You have learned, sometimes the hard way, the cost of ignoring biblical principles and directives. You know God's power because you have seen him work in and through you. You understand the complexity of leadership situations because you have lived through them, and you see God's activity more clearly in hindsight than you did in the moment. And you share what you have learned with those who inherit your legacy.

Wisdom. You have accumulated wisdom—both learned and earned. Communicating it appropriately extends your legacy to a future generation. This doesn't mean you sermonize on every subject like a boorish know-it-all who annoys people with endless stories. It means, first of all, that you live your convictions. What people will remember most after your death is how you lived, what you modeled, and the example you set. It also means communicating your wisdom legacy in meaningful ways.

Communicating legacy requires anticipating teachable moments and humbly sharing what you know. It may mean, like Peter, you write what you have learned. One friend writes occasional letters to his grandchildren in a series called "Letters from Papa." Some are humorous anecdotes from his early years—like dating stories, money missteps, and family foul-ups. Others are more serious as he addresses life issues and offers counsel. Another friend follows her grandchildren on social media, and privately e-mails or texts them short encouraging notes about life concerns revealed in their public posts. One ministry leader is taking a more passive approach. He has kept a journal for years—private for now, but a gift to his family upon his death. He's recording his faith journey, the good and the bad, with a view toward helping the next generations of his family learn from his experiences. This kind of journaling can be a profound gift. While we lack a lengthy journal because of his untimely death, my father-in-law's college journal is one of our most prized possessions. His sermon notes and personal comments reveal the legacy he left his daughter, my wife, which she is living up to in honor of her father's memory.

People. A second aspect of legacy-leaving is the people you influence—those who will outlive you and carry on what you have taught them. Whether a congregation of thousands, a company employing hundreds, or one grandchild you pour yourself into—your influence on others extends your life-impact into future generations.

The most important impact you can make on another person is facilitating their commitment to Jesus as Lord and Savior. When you do this, you make an eternal impact, not just a generational impact. Beyond that, when you help a person live in a manner obedient to Jesus, their changed life results in better opportunities for people related to them. For example, when a workaholic becomes a Christian and invests himself in his children, their lives will become more emotionally secure. When a drunkard adopts sobriety, her newfound stability makes a more positive future possible for her family. Investing yourself in helping others know Jesus and live for him improves lives now, in the future, and forever. People committed to and living for Jesus become your living legacy.

Convictions. Finally, your legacy lives on in the convictions you model. So much about life is more caught than taught. It's hard to put into words all that you have learned. It's also hard to know when and how to communicate best with others. Rest assured, however, your family and followers are watching you. They respect your leadership and are learning from your example. One of my mentors (he would have never owned that title—he was too humble) never told me much about building a healthy family. Even when I asked his secret to a strong extended family, he simply shrugged and said, "Just love 'em, I guess." He wasn't eloquent, but his example was elegant. He consistently modeled loving his wife, his adult children, and his grandchildren. I was mesmerized by his example, watched him closely, and am still trying to copy him. When he died, my heart broke in grief over his death and for the loss of the wisdom his example could have provided for years to come. I lost my guide for navigating late middle age/early senior adulthood. I still miss him, even though he died more than a decade ago. What an example he was! How much it would help me today if I could have watched him for the past ten years.

Peter left his legacy in all three ways outlined in the definition above. He was an example to the church and the convictions he modeled lived on in their collective memory. He influenced people by introducing them to Jesus and guiding them to live for him. (This is evidenced by the recipients of his two letters.) He also left behind his accumulated wisdom—two letters summarizing key messages he wanted to communicate to his followers. And in the providence of God, all of us for all time have also benefited from His wisdom. None of us are in Peter's league. Rest assured, you won't write any Scripture, but your legacy is vitally important to someone. Your family, your followers, and people who are inspired by the memory of the convictions you lived out over your lifetime will all benefit from your threefold legacy.

You may think it arrogant to even consider that you have a legacy, much less that you should record or communicate it. Please don't allow false humility to short-circuit this important concluding phase of your leadership life cycle. As you move from leading to legacy-leaving, do so with a profound sense of destiny. You can impact others, both in this season and in the future, more profoundly than you might imagine.

As you leave your legacy, keep these simple steps in mind. First, communicate your accumulated wisdom. Write and speak about how God has led you, taught you, and changed you over a lifetime. Be gentle: look for teachable moments. Be creative: wisdom shared by text message may connect with your grandkids. Be subtle: nobody likes lectures from Grandpa or guilt trips from Grandma. Find appealing ways to share your story with others. Don't be so in-your-face that you repel instead of attract them. Be realistic: you aren't going to share everything you know; not everyone will appreciate what you have to offer; and sometimes you just need to be quiet.

Second, consider writing or recording your thoughts, particularly for your family, as part of your legacy for them. Keep a journal, save marked-up Bibles, and preserve important family mementos. If you aren't a writer, consider making a video or audio recording. One of my prized possessions is a video of my grandmother recounting our family's history. With some prompting, she not only told the official history, but also the down and dirty part (which in our case is most of the story). As part of this video, she also shared some of the important lessons she had learned about life. It's a valued heirloom of a simple woman's perspective on God, family, and life.

Finally, model your convictions to the end. Finish strong. During this leadership season, your children are now adults, watching you and learning from your example. They see how you are handling life twenty or thirty years ahead of where they will be someday. Your grandchildren are also watching you, determining if what you believe really works and if you will stand by it to the end. They may be going through a rebellious phase, rolling their eyes when you try to talk to them or shutting you out altogether—but they are watching. Your other followers, many of whom have known you for years, are also loyally learning from you. Make sure you live your convictions to the end. Model what you believe as a living legacy.

Peter communicated a written legacy—two biblical books called 1 and 2 Peter. In those short letters, he summarized his accumulated wisdom and stated his most profound life convictions. The date of his writings underscores his longevity and faithfulness as a church leader. Peter's written legacy accomplishes two things. First, it models leaving a living legacy of the wisdom you've accumulated over a lifetime of learning and leading. Second, his legacy teaches us. It does for many of us what we hope our legacy will do for a few. As you read through this section, keep both of these purposes in mind. Note both his model of legacy-leaving and the legacy itself that Peter left. Both format and content are instructive.

This section, like the first two sections, isn't a thorough commentary. We make no attempt at detailed exegesis of 1 and 2 Peter. We are still taking the "big question" approach, only now we are asking, "What are the broad convictions that Peter wrote about after a lifetime of leadership?" rather than the previous questions, "What was Peter learning about leadership?" or "What do Peter's actions reveal about leadership?" To answer this third macro-level question, let's turn our attention to the record of Peter's living legacy—his convictions maintained, his wisdom accumulated, and the people he influenced for the glory of God.

This section also continues the pattern of presenting one key leadership insight, this time from Peter's books. After each chapter, there are reflection questions to help you personalize this material. There is also a question to help you connect the leadership convictions in this section to the leadership priorities in section two. Let's get started on the final season—leaving your leadership legacy.

Conviction 1

JESUS IS ENOUGH

1 Peter 1:1–12

 Early Christians, in churches scattered throughout what is modern-day Turkey, early Christians were discovering how difficult it was to follow Jesus. Peter described them as "temporary residents," which seems too soft a translation. They were exiles, nomads, pilgrims, and foreigners—made for a heavenly home but stuck here in the midst of opposition and turmoil. What kind of problems did these believers face? They were being mistreated because of their faith. They were being persecuted because of their beliefs; they suffered for their commitment to Jesus. They endured verbal abuse, physical hardship, and even death as daily threats. Peter identified with their pain and encouraged them with a core principle he had learned over a lifetime of living with similar threats. When the pressure is on and life hangs in the balance—have confidence in Jesus, no matter what!

Jesus Christ is the predominant theme for the first section of Peter's first letter. He claimed to be an "apostle of Jesus Christ" and reminded the recipients they were set apart by "the blood of Jesus Christ." Peter offered praise to God, the "Father of our Lord Jesus Christ" and underscored that their hope for thriving while suffering was "through the resurrection of Jesus Christ." He promised the recipients that their future was secure and that all things would be made right at "the revelation of Jesus Christ." In summary, Peter reminded his fellow believers that Jesus had initiated his apostleship and had redeemed them through his blood, secured them in the midst of suffering, and guaranteed their ultimate victory in heaven. Truly, Jesus Christ can be trusted in all life-threatening situations.

Christians around the world still face persecution for their faith. In these dark times, their sustaining power comes from having confidence that Jesus will deliver them, either from death or through it to an eternal reward. One persecuted leader told me of repeated interrogations and death threats. Each time he was arrested, he naturally feared for his family, his congregants, and his future ministry. But when those feelings seemed overwhelming, his solace and strength came from his relationship with Jesus. His stories of Jesus' miraculous comfort, intervention, and deliverance are humbling to hear. Jesus can be trusted through the darkest times in life.

For most Western leaders, persecution (the backdrop of Peter's writings) isn't a common threat. While these leaders may be pressured and sometimes harassed for their faith, they aren't physically attacked or otherwise made to suffer. As an American Christian leader, it embarrasses me when people lament about how the American church is being persecuted. It isn't. To claim otherwise is a disservice to the suffering church around the world. Let's be honest—our opponents are often annoying and bothersome, but they are almost never life-threatening.

Besides persecution, are there other life situations God uses to teach us the important principle of trusting Jesus when all else fails? The answer is yes. Many leaders have been through a dark night of the soul—an experience so terrifying and devoid of hope that it reduced us to utter, complete dependence on and confidence in Jesus. For some, it may be a leadership challenge like being fired from a ministry position. For others, it might be relational turmoil or a health crisis.

In 1994, I was diagnosed with thyroid cancer. While that form of cancer is largely curable, my surgeries proved the most challenging part of the process. For several reasons, my treatment plan resulted in two surgeries just five days apart. While the first surgery was relatively routine, the second was anything but!

Five days after my first surgery, supposedly exploratory, my surgeon called with the devastating news—I had cancer. He told me to go to the hospital that afternoon for surgery that evening. Since he was opening up the same area, inflamed and swollen from the previous surgery, his greatest concern was preserving my laryngeal nerves. He told me there was a chance I would never speak again. For someone who communicates for a living, this was frightening news. Thinking about possible "last words" was ominous. I told my wife and school-age children, "If this is the last thing I ever say to you, remember it forever—I love you."

The immediate recovery from surgery was difficult. My normal bodily functions shut down. Without going into too many details, all systems were either nonfunctional or on some kind of monitor because my physicians were concerned about my deteriorating condition. Two particular side effects were most challenging.

One side effect of thyroid surgery is potential damage to your parathyroid. These little glands regulate your body's absorption of calcium. While most people think calcium means strong bones, it's also an important mineral for nerve transmission throughout your body. When you are low in calcium, you lose feeling in your fingers and toes. After that, you get facial tics. These are signs your body is shutting down the extremities and saving calcium for more important functions like your heart and lungs. My first conscious thought after surgery was, "Why won't my hands stop tingling and my face stop twitching?" Then I heard the nurse explaining to my wife the calcium-filled syringe on a tray next to my bed. If my calcium levels plunged any lower, they would save my life with an immediate injection. Not the best news to hear when you are waking up from anesthesia!

My second thought was, "What's wrong with my neck?" It was swollen grotesquely, made worse by a massive bandage immobilizing my head. Attempts to speak were painful, plus, I wasn't even sure I was able to talk. The fear of trying and possibly finding out I was mute was overwhelming. Normally, I talk a lot. Not that night, as I lay there in subdued silence.

I wanted to pray, but my mind was so muddled I couldn't string any thoughts together. I tried to remember Scripture—anything to get me moving spiritually in the right direction. The only verse I could remember was "weeping lasts for the night, but joy comes in the morning" (Ps. 30:5, paraphrased). The only prayer I could pray was, "Lord, get me through to morning."

The night passed slowly. After saying my short Scripture and prayer, I dozed off. When I awoke, I thought, "Maybe it's close to morning." Then I would look at the clock and three minutes had passed. This pattern went on all night—I would remember my one memory verse, silently pray my one-sentence prayer, doze off, wake up hopeful, see the clock, feel panic that only minutes had passed, quote my verse, pray my prayer, doze off, and so on. It was the longest night of my life.

Finally, I woke up and saw sunlight. Morning! I responded to my wife's first question by saying my name. I could talk! My hands felt normal and my face wasn't twitching! When my mind cleared, I silently prayed something like this:

Lord, last night was the worst night of my life. My health was broken, my body wasn't working. I was helpless. My family and church friends could do nothing for me. My academic degrees were worthless. My talents for speaking and leading were useless. Lord, last night I couldn't even pray a good prayer. Last night, I was reduced to just one thing—You. And, Lord, I found out that you are enough.

A few years later, my wife was reflecting on that pivotal night in the hospital. She told me, "I'm not sure all that happened to you that night. But you changed more in one night than in the fifteen years I had known you before that night. When you came home from the hospital, you were a different man."

That dark night of my soul seared this reality into me: When there's nothing left in life but Jesus, he's enough. He really is. Since that night, many things that formerly overwhelmed, angered, or consumed me just haven't been important any more. Like Peter, my living legacy starts with a foundational conviction about the sufficiency of Jesus. When threatened by persecution, illness, or daunting leadership challenges—Jesus is enough. When no human resource, accomplishment, or talent can help you—Jesus is enough. When you are abused or used; when you are empty and alone—Jesus is enough. This one conviction is almost a life-legacy by itself. No matter what, have confidence in Jesus.

Questions for Reflection

1. What has God allowed you to go through to learn that Jesus is enough? If so, how has that experience changed you?
2. Why is the sufficiency of Jesus an important legacy for leaders?
3. How can you communicate this conviction through your unique story as part of your leadership legacy?
4. Which of Peter's leadership priorities might have helped form this part of his legacy?

Conviction 2

PURSUE PURITY—PERSONALLY AND IN RELATIONSHIP WITH OTHERS

1 Peter 1:13–2:10

 Personal purity and transparency in relationships with others is a challenging aspect of leaving a legacy. In our debauched world, living a moral life sounds like an old-fashioned anachronism or an impossible dream. Pornography is available, immediately, with just a few computer clicks. Sexual perversions of every kind are celebrated throughout our culture. Homosexual lifestyle choices, formerly marginalized, are now trumpeted as equal to or preferred over heterosexual behavior. Cohabitation is an accepted alternative to marriage. Moral purity has never been more difficult to maintain.

Likewise, in our self-absorbed world, prioritizing right relationships with others—at the expense of self-gratification—also seems out of touch. As some people age, they become more and more determined to have their say and get their way. One older woman told me, "After eighty, I started saying whatever I [blankety-blank] well pleased, and everyone else can just deal with it." Healthy relationships, as part of legacy-leaving, are devalued by people who think aging is an excuse for imprudent behavior.

As part of his legacy, Peter wrote about the priority of personal holiness and relational integrity in strong terms. He called on believers to leave behind "the desires of [their] former ignorance" and "be holy in all your conduct." He set the bar high by quoting God who mandates, "Be holy, because I am holy." Peter reminded his readers that they were "redeemed from [their] empty way of life" and should now model a purified life enabled by Jesus' resurrection power.

But Peter went a step further than demanding moral purity as the measure of healthy relationships. He also insisted on integrity in interpersonal relationships. He insisted that believers have been "purified . . . for sincere love of the brothers" meaning we should "love one another earnestly from a pure heart." This requires ridding "yourselves of all malice, all deceit, hypocrisy, envy, and all slander." Peter underscored the importance of healthy relationships with several metaphors—he said the believers were living stones that were being built into a spiritual house; they were a chosen race, a royal priesthood, and a holy nation—all of which speak of an integrated, supportive community.

Maintaining right relationships, including (but also broader than) personal moral purity, is an essential part of preserving your legacy. Transparency with others, keeping short accounts of wrongs committed, letting love cover egregious behavior, and sacrificing personal preferences to strengthen interpersonal relationships is challenging. Peter reminds us that purity in moral choices and interpersonal relationships is vital for leaders. Further, he underscored how doing these things are essential for leaving a legacy of Christian leadership that impacts future generations. How so?

First, a lifetime of effective leadership can be undone with a momentary lapse in moral judgment. A pastor with a long track record of faithful service became discouraged. He turned to pornography for solace and release. When evidence of the habit showed up on a church computer, he was dismissed for violating the trust of his congregation. Another national leader, after decades of service, lost his position when he succumbed to sexual temptation by hiring an escort service. These weren't young men, caught up in unrestrained passion. They were veteran leaders, nearing retirement, ensnared by immoral choices while lonely, depressed, or stressed. Moral failure, often considered a temptation for the young and virile, is an ever-present problem for leaders at every stage of life.

Finishing strong, with your moral choices reflecting personal holiness, is an essential part of your living legacy. Don't forfeit your leadership legacy for a few fleeting moments of selfish pleasure. As you move through the legacy-leaving stage of life, redouble your efforts to maintain the habits of personal holiness you have practiced over the years. Don't lose your vigilance about moral choices.

Second, a legacy of effective leadership is preserved by the healthy relationships you leave behind. Put another way, part of your leadership legacy is the people you have trained and the future impact they will have because of your influence through them. One leader unraveled years of effective service by torching his most meaningful relationships in the final years of his tenure. He allowed impatience and anger to overwhelm good judgment. His time-is-short attitude caused him to bulldoze through people who opposed his final initiatives. Rather than leaving a legacy of effective service, represented by strong relationships and a healthy commitment to carry on his emphases, he left behind the rubble of a fractured organization. His followers no longer revered him when he finally retired; instead, they resented him. As you draw closer to the end of your active leadership role, remember, relationships matter—a lot. Don't undo years of effective ministry by running roughshod over people to finish your final, self-serving agenda.

For more than forty years, Cecil Sims was an influential leader among Baptists in the Pacific Northwest. To say he was an energetic leader would be like calling the Mount St. Helens eruption a hiccup. He was a dynamo, a perpetual wellspring of spiritual energy, creative ideas, and passionate service. It was my privilege to follow him in the leadership role from which he retired. People warned me, some even commiserated with me, about how hard it would be to put up with Cecil. The opposite turned out to be true.

Cecil spent a few weeks orienting me to my new job. He then offered to be on call for the first year, doing what he could behind the scenes to help me. I called him often. He went out of his way to honor me, speak well of my leadership, and convince his peers to give the young man a chance. He supported me and helped make me a more successful leader. To the surprise of many, his service became so valuable that we added him back to our ministry staff in a volunteer role. We covered his expenses as he traveled the Northwest for several years, in retirement, helping church leaders with various special projects, primarily in stewardship development.

After a few years, an interesting transition took place. People around the Northwest spoke often about how Cecil had handled retirement and how he had supported me." His stature as a leader increased after he left his formal leadership role. Many of his longtime friends—the same people who had cautioned me about Cecil's tendency to meddle—became his most vocal admirers. Younger leaders were inspired by his example of humility and care in nurturing our relationship as well as other relationships with other younger, emerging leaders. Like Cecil, when you maintain relational integrity to the end of your life, your leadership legacy will be strengthened. When you go out of your way to build others up and honor your successors, rather than undermine their efforts, your post-retirement leadership may be your most important contribution.

Getting older doesn't give you permission to speak your mind any more than when you were younger. Preserving relationships and patiently fostering the next generation, rather than criticizing their new ways, reveals statesmanship. Your leadership legacy depends on how you treat people, right up to the end of your life.

When Cecil died, there was no relief that a meddlesome detractor was finally gone. Instead, there was a profound sense of loss. I had lost a mentor and friend. We had all lost a role model for nurturing younger leaders. His care for me, deference to me, and support for me were a significant blessing. Because of his graciousness in building our relationship, my leadership was more effective and his legacy more defined. Hundreds turned out for his memorial service, and several speakers magnified his contribution after retirement as his greatest leadership legacy. His stature had grown as he nurtured leadership relationships in his later years.

Your leadership legacy must include moral purity as a significant way of maintaining healthy relationships. Beyond that, relational integrity and transparency must also part of your legacy. How you treat people in your later years largely determines how you will be remembered. You can either magnify what you have previously accomplished or wash away those positive memories by mistreating people. This is more than aging gracefully. It's making an intentional decision to relate well to the people replacing you. It's choosing to inspire them to greater effectiveness rather than critique them for supposedly messing up what you accomplished.

QUESTIONS FOR REFLECTION

1. How will you maintain moral purity in the legacy phase of leadership?
2. What are some relational challenges in the legacy phase of life? How will you intentionally build relationships to honor the next generation of leaders?
3. How can you communicate this conviction as part of your leadership legacy?
4. Which of Peter's leadership priorities might have helped form this part of his legacy?

BUILD GOOD RELATIONSHIPS

1 Peter 2:11–3:12

 After describing the importance of living a holy life, both morally and with integrity in relationships, Peter devoted a considerable part of his written legacy to applying those foundational truths to various kinds of relationships. Part of his legacy was calling believers to apply the Christian ethic in three significant areas—governing authorities, vocational networks, and family structures. He recognized the public nature of the Christian faith and how it must impact communities and families to genuinely make a difference.

Peter admonished his followers to "abstain from fleshly desires" and "conduct yourselves honorably among the Gentiles" so that by "observing your good works" they will "glorify God." He recognized that Christianity, a marginalized sect in his day, would be legitimized by how its followers acted in public. Peter wanted them to model their faith, by allowing God's transformative power to be revealed behaviorally—and not just as an internal conversion experience. This is still wise counsel today—which is why it's included as part of Peter's permanent written legacy. Christians are still marginalized in many places. Relating properly in the public square—to the government, in the workplace, and in their family—validates their faith.

Peter told his persecuted followers to "submit to every human author-ity," including the "Emperor as the supreme authority or to governors as those sent out by him." Peter acknowledged the freedom Christians have through ultimate allegiance to God, but tempered that with instructions to not "use your freedom as a way to conceal evil." Freedom is for doing good, not creating problems for governing authorities. This was particularly challenging since Christianity enjoyed no favorable status with govern-ments at the time. Relating positively with authorities in a democracy, with its accompanying freedoms, is much easier than relating well with abusive governing structures. Peter's legacy was written in the face of hostility and persecution, which underscores the value of his advice even more.

Peter then gave similar instructions to a special group—Christian slaves. This is a difficult subject to translate into the modern context. Christians abhor slavery and should work to end it completely. It's rep-rehensible and must be stopped, in every form and place. In the first century, however, first-generation Christians didn't have the political or moral influence to make that happen. As a concession to that reality, Peter told Christian slaves to "submit with all fear to your masters" even when it meant suffering unjustly, believing that "when you do what is good and suffer, if you endure it, this brings favor with God." Slavery was a common economic and vocational reality for early Christians. While a one-for-one parallel isn't advisable, the principle taught here has some application for working in vocational settings today. Christians must find ways to relate effectively to their employers. Doing so, even while demanding bet-ter working conditions or other appropriate changes, demonstrates your Christian ethic in the workplace.

Finally, Peter called on wives to submit to their husbands—and in particular, unbelieving or rebellious husbands—who might be influenced for good by their patient example. His instructions emphasize inner character over outer beauty and the importance of making holy choices rather than maintaining a haughty appearance. Husbands received similar instructions on relating to their wives. Peter told them to give their wives honor as fellow believers, in contrast to the demeaning way most women were treated in those days. Christian domestic relationships, in contrast to the cultural mores, should demonstrate the value of both partners in mar-riage. Modeling those behaviors was a stark demonstration of the impact of the gospel.

Understanding these specific instructions for relating to governing authorities, vocational networks, and family structures is vital—but what's the overall message Peter left through this part of his legacy? The over-arching message is that building healthy relationships throughout your community demonstrates the authenticity of the Christian faith. When your actions reveal Jesus, your words about him will receive a much more receptive hearing.

Put most simply, people matter. Developing meaningful relationships in your community, at work, and in your home produces a more lasting impact than accomplishing almost any project. People matter more than projects.

In my early leadership years, my perspective on relationships was skewed. Two misperceptions drove me. First, I saw people as a means to an end. I considered my task as a leader the responsibility to use, manage, and otherwise deploy people to accomplish my vision. People were assets, yes, but mostly as cogs in the ministry production process. Second, I often saw people as an impediment to my effectiveness. People who were uncoop-erative, opinionated, or otherwise disruptive to my agenda were "problem people." They either needed to repent or leave; either way, they needed to get out of my way. My warped view of relationships was destructive and painful for everyone, including me.

Fortunately, God and some courageous Christians were unwilling to leave my perspective unchallenged. God continually thwarted my driven-ness, causing people to get in my way and slow me down on a regular basis. Deacons and other church leaders confronted my callous attitude toward people, demanded improved relational skills, and modeled healthier pat-terns for me. I'm slow sometimes, but eventually the message sank in. People are the ministry. Relationships are essential to effective ministry. Connecting with people and influencing them for good is a primary strat-egy for success. Abusing people to accomplish my agenda, no matter how high and holy it sounded, was counterproductive. God expected me to work with and through people, prioritizing their growth and development, rather than simply using them to fulfill my ambitions.

Why is it so hard to prioritize people over projects? Why is working with people at all levels—in public, at work, and at home—so difficult? The answers are many and complex, but the core problem is confusion about our purpose. At its most basic level, Christian leadership is about helping people change—it is not just about getting things done. For Christian leaders, our priority should be helping people to develop as disciples who reflect the image of Jesus Christ. Getting projects done may be the means to the end, but it isn't the end. The end—and the beginning and middle—of Christian leadership is getting people to commit to and become more like Jesus.

Keeping this priority in view is challenging. Leaders are activists with long to-do lists. We are execution specialists, known for walking the walk, not talking the talk. But think about this. Does God really need you to get anything done? After all, he spoke and the universe came into existence. Obviously, he doesn't need you to do anything for him. As a leader, then, your assignments and activities are God's laboratory for shaping you—and your followers—into the image of Jesus. Leadership is about relationship. It's about your relationship with God, your relationship with your followers, and their relationships with God, you, and each other. Keeping this priority in view is what Peter focused on when writing his legacy letter.

Peter himself related in all three arenas—government, work, and home. He had multiple interactions with governmental leaders (rulers and military officials), navigated various vocational relationships (fishing partners in his former life, peers like Paul in ministry), and managed domestic challenges (like an ailing mother-in-law—which indicates he was married). Although Peter had many ministry accomplishments, like preaching at Pentecost, helping lead the Jerusalem church, witnessing and performing miracles, and being one of the closest earthly companions of Jesus, when it came to emphasizing what really matters in ministry leadership, he focused on the importance of relationships over accomplishments.

Build good relationships, not just as a means to get more done, but because relationships are the track on which true ministerial progress is made. The ultimate outcome for Christian leaders is changed lives. The way to change lives is through healthy relationships. People matter more than projects or products. Leave a strong legacy by relating well in public, at work, and in your home. People will remember you more for impacting those relationships than for any task you may accomplish along the way.

Questions for Reflection

1. Why do relationships matter so much for Christian leaders? Do you value people more than projects? If not, why not?
2. Where is it most difficult to show your faith—in public, at work, or among your family members? Why?
3. How can you communicate this conviction as part of your leadership legacy?
4. Which of Peter's leadership priorities might have helped form this part of his legacy?

Conviction 4

DO THE RIGHT THING

1 Peter 3:13–4:19

 As you near the end of your leadership career, you will likely look back over a mixed bag of decisions—some good, some bad. You will also look back over countless situations where you chose a course of action when the options were muddled and the consequences unclear. In other cases, the situation was more traumatic and defined. You had to make choices with significant negative results assured—like losing your job, downsizing others, losing money, creating divisions in your ministry, or some other negative result. In the worst possible cases, people suffered because of your decisions.

Leaders make decisions, sometimes hard decisions, in the face of turmoil or even persecution. Part of leading is taking responsibility for making tough choices and living with the consequences. One friend told me, "You can't lead if you can't inflict pain." Our decisions may cause pain for others. At other times, we afflict ourselves by our leadership decisions. Leading hurts.

How can a leader maintain emotional equilibrium, knowing the potential consequences of the choices made? What helps maintain perspective and gives you the strength to make the hard calls? Can you leave a legacy of controversial decisions with generally good outcomes? Peter outlined resources for leaders to draw on when making tough decisions to do the right thing, no matter the anticipated negative consequences.

Peter started this part of his legacy with a promise that "if you should suffer for righteousness, you are blessed." He advocates being ready to "give a defense" of our hope in Jesus Christ and responding to everyone with "gentleness and respect, keeping your conscience clear." Peter advised that detractors will ultimately be "put to shame," although in the short run they may appear victorious. He reminds us "it is better to suffer for doing good, if that should be God's will, than for doing evil."

Throughout this section, Peter interweaves the example of Jesus making the right decisions and suffering for it as a model for us. Jesus did the right thing and suffered for it in more profound ways than any of us will ever experience. He chose to die for us; he suffered for sin he didn't commit to make our salvation possible. His example is the ultimate illustration of a person suffering unjustly while steadfastly refusing to compromise doing what was right. By following Jesus' example, you can "equip yourselves also with the same resolve" to resist the "slander" that comes from people who attack you for making right choices with controversial results.

Along with Jesus' example, Peter highlights two other resources to help you make those hard decisions with painful consequences. He begins by reminding us to "be serious and disciplined for prayer." He then advocates, "Above all, maintain an intense love for each other, since love covers a multitude of sins." Peter insisted that strength is drawn from prayer and from other believers, people who will stand with you when the chips are down. Some people will abandon you to suffer alone. But others, who truly love you, will stand with you no matter how difficult the situation becomes. Peter reminds us to foster fellowship with other believers as a resource to strengthen us through difficult decision-making.

Prior to the reminder about the support of others, Peter mentioned the priority of prayer. Your relationship with God, as accessed through prayer, is your primary resource when deciding to do what's right no matter the consequence. When you face a formidable decision, pray about it. When you feel isolated and alone and you're not sure who to turn to, God is there for you. Pray about your decision, make your best choice, and God will sustain you in the darkest moments.

The secondary resource for strength in tough decision-making is the love and support of special believers. While many people will abandon you when pressure-packed situations become overwhelming, some will stand firm. When I became a seminary president a few years ago, a friend sent me this note: "When times get tough, call on Jesus. Then call on me. I will be there for you." And he has been! Good friends who will stand with you, who understand the no-win situations you must face, who trust your character to undergird good decisions, and who refuse to abandon you are a special gift from God. Fair-weather followers may cut and run at the first sign of trouble. True friends will stand with you to the end.

Despite these resources—prayer and supportive friends—choosing to do the right thing no matter the consequences is still difficult. One reason is that the results of these decisions often look like failures in the short run. One pastor stood up to racism in his church and lost his job. Years later, his moral conviction was celebrated as the church repented and welcomed members of other races. One executive made an unpopular decision to change the funding priorities and policies of his organization. Short-term pain made many squeal for relief. But when an economic downturn put many other organizations out of business, his weathered the storm without layoffs or cutbacks. He went from goat to hero, praised by the same employees who had griped about his austerity in better times. One academic leader defended a key doctrinal position, which cost him followers and dollars. His school ultimately recovered but not without years of struggle. In all these cases, the right decision produced immediate loss and personal pain. While the rest of the story is more positive, in those moments of decision and immediate aftermath, the results weren't assured.

This is reality—many hard decisions produce immediate pain. We hope righteousness will ultimately prevail, but when the decision is made, there's no guarantee about the future outcome. The challenge is in doing the right thing no matter the consequences or results. The most dramatic biblical example is the story of Shadrach, Meshach, and Abednego, as told in Daniel 3.

Nebuchadnezzar was king of Babylon. He erected a huge golden statue of himself and demanded that everyone worship it. But when the signal was given, there were three young men who refused to bow down before the idol. Nebuchadnezzar was furious. He threatened to toss Shadrach,

Meshach, and Abednego into a fiery furnace. Their response perfectly summarizes this part of Peter's legacy: "If the God we serve exists, then He can rescue us from the furnace of blazing fire, and He can rescue us from the power of you, the king. But even if He does not rescue us, we want you as king to know that we will not serve your gods or worship the gold statue you set up" (Dan. 3:17–18). These men were determined to do the right thing—no matter what.

They refused to worship an idol and were tossed into a furnace so hot their captors were killed in the process. Yes, they were later delivered by God's power—but that's not the most significant part of the story. The key point is that these young men were determined to do the right thing whether deliverance happened or not.

Part of your leadership legacy is the decisions you make and their results. More important, your legacy will show the kind of decisions you made and your moral courage to do the right thing no matter the consequences. Peter modeled this with some of his decisions, for example, like deciding the doctrine of salvation at the Jerusalem Council and accepting the vision of the descending sheets as indication of God's inclusion of the Gentiles in his kingdom. Peter knew the pressure of strategic decision-making and the ensuing controversies in the church. When he wrote this part of his legacy, he challenged us to follow his example.

You will leave a legacy of strategic decisions. Some of these may be quite personal—who you married and how you managed your finances. Some will be part of your leadership role—where you served, the ministry you built, the convictions you upheld, the doctrine you defended, and the people you employed. All of these decisions contribute to your legacy. But more important, the quality of your decisions—your willingness to consistently do the right thing no matter the consequences—is your true legacy. People will remember what you did and what you decided. But they will remember more what you stood for along the way.

QUESTIONS FOR REFLECTION

1. How do prayer and the example of Jesus sustain you through difficult decision-making? How does the support of faithful friends also help?

2. When have you made a difficult decision to do the right thing no matter the consequences? What were the short-term results? The long-term results?

3. How can you communicate this conviction as part of your leadership legacy?

4. Which of Peter's leadership priorities might have helped form this part of his legacy?

Conviction 5

BE STEADFAST

1 Peter 5:1–14

 Peter concluded his first letter with pointed, stirring words written directly to pastoral leaders. This part of his legacy underscores the importance of church leaders and their opportunity to impact many believers. Given the brevity of Peter's written legacy, the significance of these instructions can't be overlooked. Singling out pastors and elders magnifies their importance. It's essential to consider what Peter wrote about them. He could have written instructions about any aspect of leadership. The specific issues he chose, then, must be very significant. While they addressed pressing issues for the recipients, they are also timeless instructions for leaders in every generation. Their inclusion in this short letter highlights their importance. If you were only able to write a hundred words or so about church leadership, what would you write? Obviously, you would address the most important lessons you had learned. Peter did that in this part of his legacy.

Peter called church leaders to specific responsibilities and exemplary behavior. He also warned them about their greatest temptation and the source of their fiercest opposition. Part of Peter's legacy was his faithfulness as a church leader. He referred to himself as a "fellow elder," emphasizing his identification with pastoral leaders more than his apostleship.

He accepted his church leadership role and all its additional expectations and fulfilled them admirably, leaving a legacy of effective service. Peter admonished other church leaders to live up to his example and beyond that, to meet the high expectations Jesus has of ministry leaders.

Given all he could have written based on his vast experiences—from walking with Jesus to preaching at Pentecost to leading in Jerusalem—what key issues did he prioritize?

Peter exhorted church leaders to "shepherd God's flock," calling to mind their primary responsibility. Pastors, or elders as they are called here, are spiritual leaders who give oversight to and develop their flock—the people of God. Pastors aren't managers, executives, presidents, or officers. Pastors are shepherds. The perpetual temptation, particularly for pastors who work in larger churches, is to trade their shepherding role for another role. While many other tasks may be added to a pastor's responsibilities, giving up their pastor's heart will always, in the end, prove detrimental. People expect to be led and fed at church; not managed, used, or treated like commodities. Peter saw far into the future, to our present day of institutionalized religion, when pastors might forget this important principle. He included "shepherd the flock" as his first priority for pastoral leadership.

Peter then addressed a second major issue for ministry leaders—being tempted by the love of money. Already, even among the poverty experienced by many first-century Christians, pastors were tempted to work for monetary gain. Today, pastoral leadership can become more a career than a calling. Some pastors are well paid, with benefits similar to or exceeding those provided employees in other professions. Being compensated as a pastor isn't wrong. Pastoring primarily for the paycheck, however, is what Peter condemns. Of all the temptations Peter could have warned against, he chose the love of money. His warning resounds through the centuries and is pertinent in every generation and culture. God's leaders must serve from higher motives, grateful for the financial support they receive but never captured by the love of money.

Peter continued with strong words about character as the foundation of ministerial success. He challenged leaders to serve humbly—indentifying humility as a required core character quality. Leaders model servanthood; "lording [their position] over those entrusted" to their care is wrong. He specifically singled out younger leaders and admonished them to work

humbly and to defer to older leaders. Peter then underscored the importance of humility by referencing Proverbs 3:34, "God resists the proud but
gives grace to the humble." All these instructions emphasize humility as a
core quality of effective leaders.

After these instructions about leadership, Peter warned about the
satanic opposition that pastors and other church leaders face. He wrote,
"Be serious! Be alert! Your adversary the Devil is prowling around like a
roaring lion, looking for anyone he can devour." Ministers face opposition,
and it's easy to forget the source—Satan! He is malicious and aggressive,
working against men and women who lead God's work. Peter could have
written about governmental, community, church, or individual opposition—all of which ministry leaders encounter from time to time. Many
leadership books, including one of mine, focus on handling these troublesome people. Peter's legacy, however, points to the true source of opposition. Ministry leaders must never forget that Satan is our primary enemy
and the source of the opposition we frequently face.

After this blunt reminder, Peter ended this section on an upbeat note.
He reminded pastoral leaders to "resist" Satan by taking the offensive in
prayer. He reminded them that they are in a common battle because "the
same sufferings are being experienced by your fellow believers throughout
the world." Peter promised ultimate victory because, in the face of satanic
opposition, Jesus "will personally restore, establish, strengthen, and support you after you have suffered a little." Notice that there will be suffering—leaders aren't exempt from that. But there will also be ultimate
victory because "dominion belongs to Him forever."

When Peter wrote these instructions to pastoral leaders as part of
his legacy, he highlighted four key points. First, he pointed out that the
primary function of pastoral leadership is shepherding people. Second, he
identified the deadening temptation for pastors/elders/ministers as the love
of money. Third, he reminded us that the foundation for leadership success
is transformed character, particularly demonstrated by humility. Fourth,
Peter clearly reminded us that the opposition to Christian leadership is
spiritual, led by Satan and executed by demonic forces.

The brevity and specificity of these instructions has confronted me
about my own teaching, speaking, and writing about leadership. These
four emphases were Peter's summation about pastoral ministry after years
of effective learning and leading. He emphasized maintaining a shepherd's

focus, resisting financial temptations, developing true character, and fighting spiritual battles. Peter's legacy, reflected in what he learned over a lifetime, convicts me to stress these points when training other leaders. Peter emphasized shepherding as a priority, the necessity of fiscal responsibility, developing character more than skills, and discerning the demonic forces behind our spiritual battles. While other issues may deserve careful treatment, these priorities cannot be ignored. They are, according to the legacy left by one of the most experienced and wisest leaders of Christian history, foundational to effective ministry.

One pastor, Dr. T. C. Melton, has modeled these qualities for about sixty years. He has steadfastly maintained a pastor's heart, reminding his protégés that personal work is the key to everything. During years of service, even in a larger church, he prioritized visiting the sick, marrying young couples, comforting the bereaved, and counseling the hurting. While associates may have helped carry the load in these areas, he always found time to be pastoral—shepherding people through the trials, challenges, and the changes life brings.

Dr. Melton never fell in love with money; he always made sure others had what they needed and his compensation was commensurate with a modest lifestyle in his community. His character was beyond reproach, he was a walking definition of the phrase "a good man," as used to describe various biblical characters (i.e., Barnabas in Acts 11:24). In his later years, Dr. Melton remained focused on the spiritual nature of Christian service, teaching that prayer focused on overcoming satanic strategies was our primary method of advancing the gospel, growing churches, and transforming people. While you have probably never met this model pastor, hopefully, you know one like him. He has given his life to making Jesus well-known, not building his own name into a brand. He has served quietly and sacrificially, grateful for the opportunity to make a difference, and satisfied with the appreciation of those he has helped.

Almost forty years ago, as a high school student, I wanted to be steadfast like Brother Melton. Now, after meeting many more well-known leaders, I still want to be like the pastor who mentored me into ministry. To be pastoral—to be known for shepherding people toward maturity in Jesus, serving with pure motives rather than for the money, being defined more by strength of character than accomplishments, and winning spiritual battles rather than fighting with people—that's the best way any ministry leader can be remembered.

QUESTIONS FOR REFLECTION

1. Do you have a pastor's heart? If not, how can you capture/recapture this ministry perspective?
2. Is the love of money motivating your leadership choices? If so, how will you overcome this temptation?
3. Have you lost focus on fighting spiritual opposition? How will you change?
4. How can you communicate this conviction as part of your leadership legacy?
5. Which of Peter's leadership priorities might have helped form this part of his legacy?

Conviction 6

TRUST JESUS

2 Peter 1:1–15

 If this chapter's theme seems familiar, it should be. When Peter wrote his second legacy letter, he returned to a theme similar to his opening words in the first one (see Conviction 1). Battle-proven and time-tested, Jesus was Peter's constant source of sustaining strength. He had delivered Peter through and from countless trials—some recorded in Scripture, many lost to human memory. In Acts, for example, Jesus was there when Peter was imprisoned for healing a lame man, with him when he stood up to the Jerusalem church about circumcision, and present when Ananias' and Sapphira's dead bodies were dragged out for burial.

We read these stories with hindsight, marveling at Peter's bravery and conviction. He experienced them in real time, however, with the accompanying fears and doubts, and all the while he trusted Jesus to sustain him in the moment. Since Acts is a selective history, what else might Peter have experienced that isn't recorded in the Bible? Probably dozens of challenges of all kinds resulting from fulfilling his various leadership responsibilities. Through it all, Peter was profoundly convinced of the sufficiency of Jesus.

Peter wrote that Jesus' "divine power has given us everything required for life and godliness" and "He has given us very great and precious promises, so that through them you may share in the divine nature, escaping the corruption that is in the world." Because of these incredible resources, Peter told believers to "make every effort to supplement your faith with goodness, goodness with knowledge, knowledge with self-control, self-control with endurance, endurance with godliness, godliness with brotherly affection, and brotherly affection with love" because "the person who lacks these things is blind and shortsighted and has forgotten the cleansing from his past sins," as accomplished by Jesus.

Peter then turned his attention to heaven, his soon-to-be-realized eternal home and the ultimate example of the sufficiency of the Savior. He admonished believers to "make every effort to confirm your calling and election, because if you do these things you will never stumble. For in this way, entry into the eternal kingdom of our Lord and Savior Jesus Christ will be richly supplied to you." Peter considered it "right, as long as I am in this bodily tent, to wake you up with a reminder, knowing that I will soon lay aside my tent, as our Lord Jesus Christ has also shown me." He concluded with the hope that "you may be able to recall these things at any time after my departure," further underscoring his sense that the end of his life was near.

One of the best things about getting older is gaining perspective. Over time, your viewpoint on past events changes. What once seemed really important now seems less so, and mountain-sized problems look like anthills in retrospect. It's hard to have perspective when you are living through conflict, your leadership is questioned, you don't know the answers to perplexing problems, or you aren't sure which direction to go. Encouraging words from leaders who have been there and done that can help. Like Peter, veteran leaders look back over their lives and see the sustaining sufficiency of Jesus. Listening to their counsel can help when you feel lost, lonely, and overwhelmed.

When I was a younger leader, we moved to Oregon to plant a church. I was trying to buy a house. The sellers wanted $1,000 more than I had offered. I was in a quandary, stewing over the problem. I had the money, but was paralyzed, not knowing if should I should pay any more. I was over-thinking and over-spiritualizing—agonizing as if this was a blip in the process or a barrier God was erecting to get me out of the deal. I was stressed out from moving and taking the church-planting risk. My confidence was shaken, and I was afraid I was about to make a huge mistake.

I called Casey, my trusted mentor. He listened and laughed. "Do it, you'll never look back," he said. I bought the house, and he was right. In hindsight, it's a bit embarrassing how such a little problem seemed so big at the time.

Why include this story? It's not an earthshaking leadership decision. Yet, this is the kind of situation that needlessly immobilizes novice leaders. As an inexperienced home-buyer trying to make what at the time was a big decision, I needed wisdom. I needed someone who had moved a few times and bought a few houses to give me perspective. In a much more profound way, that's what Peter writes in this part of his legacy. He is telling us (my paraphrase), "Listen, no matter what you are facing, Jesus is sufficient. I've been through just about everything you can think of, and Jesus proved himself more than adequate over and over again."

Like my home-buying story above, leadership challenges are more difficult because we are living through them for the first time, in real time. Life isn't a dress rehearsal; it's a live performance. You lead live; there's no video replay possible. Whether you are facing angry church leaders, out-of-control bloggers, or a multimillion-dollar building decision, you don't get a dry run before the real thing has to be faced and resolved. Spiritual resources like faith, peace, and wisdom are available in Jesus Christ. Remembering this, and accessing all he offers, is the challenge. Reading counsel from Peter can help. Asking veteran leaders for perspective can also help. Both are valid means to finding hindsight perspective on real-time challenges.

Peter then introduces another important perspective-generating theme. He writes, in direct and poignant fashion, about heaven, calling it "the eternal kingdom of our Lord and Savior Jesus Christ." He used interesting imagery—a tent—to describe his earthly body. He claimed a premonition about his death, "as our Lord Jesus Christ has also shown me," when he would "lay aside [his] tent." By this time, Peter's body was probably showing the wear and tear of a long life. Putting it bluntly, he was becoming an old man—hairy ears, potbelly, receding hairline, and frequent trips to the bathroom. Time marches on and tramples all in its path. The sin-marred human body can only last so long. Peter had a sense that his tent had about fulfilled its purpose and would soon be cast aside.

Many believers, including some leaders, give lip service to belief in heaven but live as if this life is all that matters. Many missionary candidates, for example, bear the pain of disappointing their parents who don't support their call. One particular couple agonized when their Christian parents told them, "You need to get a ministry position near us and raise our grandchildren close by. Serving overseas is for other people's children." Living apart from family is painful enough, much less when this kind of guilt-tripping is involved.

When our children took jobs around the world, we felt this same sense of loss, but we were buttressed by the finality and eternity of heaven. Life is short. Heaven is long. Separation for the sake of the gospel is difficult but essential for obedient Christians to extend the message to people who have never heard the name of Jesus.

Peter's moving description of preparing to set aside his tent reminds us that life is transitory and brief. We have, if we live a long time, about fifty years to make an eternal impact—and then we will have eons to enjoy the results. Sure, separation from children and grandchildren is painful. They are part of our legacy—but not the only part. The core of your legacy is living in radical obedience to Jesus, motivating others (including your family) by your words and example to obey Jesus, enjoying the transgenerational impact after your life is over, and then eternity together with everyone who enjoys heaven, at least in part, because you lived. Life is short; heaven is long. Don't forget that! Keeping this reality in mind is the ultimate perspective-provider on the challenges, difficulties, and problems of leadership.

QUESTIONS FOR REFLECTION

1. When have you experienced the sufficiency of Jesus? How does this memory give you perspective?
2. Who do you turn to when you need to gain perspective on a problem you are facing?
3. How does the reality of heaven change the way you are leading?
4. How can you communicate this conviction as part of your leadership legacy?
5. Which of Peter's leadership priorities might have helped form this part of his legacy?

Conviction 7

TRUST THE WORD OF GOD

2 Peter 1:16–21, 3:15–17

 There have never been more words spoken, written, and recorded than right now. Even if you read this book twenty years after it's published, the previous sentence will still be true. New forms of media have exploded onto the scene, and the changes show no sign of letting up anytime soon. Words matter, but sorting out which ones really matter is getting more and more difficult. Just how many blogs, websites, books, articles, podcasts, and other media can you really consume? Peter anticipated this problem and gave an important directive as he neared the end of his life: he implored believers to heed the Word of God.

Peter lived in an interesting time related to the Word of God. He had access to the written word—the Old Testament—and used it regularly. Evidence of this includes his use of Old Testament texts in his sermons, as recorded in Acts and in quotations in his legacy letters. Peter also delivered words from God—his sermons and other public comments as they were later written by Luke and canonized as Scripture in Acts. Peter also recognized that Scripture was being written by his contemporaries, specifically Paul, who Peter claimed "has written to you according to the wisdom given him. He speaks about these things in all his letters in which there are some matters that are hard to understand." That's refreshing—some of Paul's writings have been considered complicated from the very beginning. Peter placed high value on Paul's writings. This is underscored by his warning that those writings had to be preserved and carefully interpreted since, "the untaught and unstable twist them to their own destruction, as they also do with the rest of the Scriptures." Peter acknowledged that Paul's writings were on par with the Old Testament. Finally, Peter also wrote Scripture, penning his legacy books known as 1 and 2 Peter.

Peter was intimately involved with the Word of God. He used the Old Testament in his ministry, spoke words that became Scripture, recognized Scripture when it was written by others, and made his own contribution to the canon. Peter based his authority to use, interpret, and create Scripture on two realities. First, he and the other apostles were "eyewitnesses of His majesty" (the resurrection). He did not, then, "follow cleverly contrived myths when we made known to you the power and coming of our Lord Jesus Christ." Peter based his authority to identify Scripture on his personal relationship with and witness of the resurrection of Jesus.

Peter also based his recognition of the Word of God on the reality that God had spoken in the past, even in Peter's presence. God had spoken at the baptism of Jesus, saying, "This is My beloved Son. I take delight in Him!" (Matt. 3:17). He had also spoken when Peter was with Jesus "on the holy mountain" (the Mount of Transfiguration). Peter was convinced that the Scriptures came from God—through men, but nonetheless from God—because he recognized God's voice. Peter had heard God's voice, literally, and recognized it when it came through others. He wrote, "No prophecy of Scripture comes from one's own interpretation, because no prophecy ever came by the will of man; instead, men spoke from God as they were moved by the Holy Spirit."

There's a lot packed into this part of Peter's legacy. Obviously, and for all the reasons just described, he highly valued the Word of God and counseled believers "to pay attention to it, as to a lamp shining in a dismal place." That's important imagery for our generation. Western culture has been profoundly influenced by the Bible for centuries. That influence, however, is rapidly waning. Darkness is expanding, and the light of the Word is lessening. Christians today have a remarkable opportunity to fulfill the mandate in Peter's legacy. We can magnify the Word of God, and in doing so, shine its bright light into the darkness of contemporary culture. We do so by interpreting the Bible correctly and living obediently according to its teachings. More than doing this individually, we also band together to do it more powerfully through Bible-based churches.

As Peter neared the end of his life, part of his culminating message was for believers to take the Word of God seriously. He had experienced this stark reality: other words fail. The plans and schemes of humankind, no matter how cleverly conceived and skillfully presented, lack the staying power of Scripture. He was instrumental during a time when part of the Word of God was being formed. He had trusted the Old Testament, he'd heard God speak audibly, had been an instrument of speaking future Scripture, he recognized Scripture being written by others, and had written some himself. Peter recognized the timeless trustworthiness of the Word of God and the importance of hearing it, above all other words.

Peter also recognized the danger of perverting the Word of God through blatant misinterpretation. He warned that people were already abusing God's instructions, as "the untaught and unstable twist them to their own destruction." Peter cautioned believers to "be on your guard, so that you are not led away by the error of lawless people and fall from your own stability." Twisting the meaning of the Bible to suit selfish purposes was already happening among the first-generation Christian leaders. How much more today!

As part of his legacy, Peter counseled leaders to take the Bible seriously—to interpret it carefully, and obey it fully. Doing so was already difficult in his generation, and is even more so in ours. We are surrounded by detractors who ignore or ridicule the Bible. While outsiders are intimidating, the greater problem, Peter acknowledges, are the so-called Christian leaders who claim to take the Bible seriously while recasting its meaning to suit their selfish purposes. The most dramatic example today is those who are using the Bible to justify changing definitions of morality, gender, and marriage. As Peter warned, "the unstable and untaught twist [the Scriptures] to their own destruction."

The saddest part of misusing Scripture on these issues (and other important topics as well) is the ultimate end—destruction. Lives are ruined when the Word of God is flaunted or ignored. Those who teach the Bible's plain meaning are often marginalized as uncaring and intolerant. The opposite is actually true. We love people so much we are willing to be ridiculed for telling the truth. We can't stand idly by while people are propelled toward catastrophe by sweet-sounding error. When false teachers win the day—whether culturally elite educators, media personalities, or erudite preachers—people who follow them are eventually destroyed. No truly caring person can tolerate such abuse. We are compelled to speak up.

Far beyond what we say to others, however, our legacy is determined more by how we respond to the Bible. Make sure you are obeying it fully, doing all it teaches, and humbly trusting its promises, despite the supposed reality of your circumstances. This is an essential part of every believer's legacy, and certainly every leader's legacy. You can leave behind the memory of a life well lived, ordered by Scripture, and confident of its outcome because of its power. The results of your godly choices, based on the Bible in contrast to cultural norms, will last into the next generation.

Consider this countercultural choice, for example, to the current confusion about morality, gender, and marriage. If you choose to live out the true biblical teaching on these subjects, there's increasing likelihood you will be ostracized. In the short run, your choices may be painful. In the long run, your family will be blessed as commitments are kept, children are reared with emotional security, men and women are both honored, and society enjoys the positive results of your choices. This is just one example of your choices leaving a legacy of obedience to Scripture, lasting beyond your lifetime. When you do this, you show your trust in the only Word that will endure forever—the Word of God. Doing so assures your legacy more than trusting any other word by any so-called authority clamoring for attention today. Your leadership legacy must rest on this firm foundation.

QUESTIONS FOR REFLECTION

1. Do you have any reservations regarding the statement that the Bible is the Word of God? Why?
2. How do you observe the Bible's message being twisted by spiritual leaders in your community? How do you respond to this?
3. What crucial areas of obedience to Scripture must you resolve to leave a positive legacy impacting future generations of your family?
4. How can you communicate this conviction as part of your leadership legacy?
5. Which of Peter's leadership priorities might have helped form this part of his legacy?

Conviction 8

CONFRONT LIES WITH TRUTH

2 Peter 2:1–22

Apologists are sometimes considered the attack dogs of modern Christianity. They seem to be on the prowl, looking for a fight. More peace-loving Christians, including some leaders, wonder why they have to be so vitriolic. Peter weighed in on this issue in a way that may surprise you. As a person ages, they often get more patient. They lose energy for fighting with others and just want to live peacefully. This might have been expected of Peter. Not so! As Peter neared the end of his written legacy (and his life), he took a strong stand, advocating in blunt terms for standing up to false teachers. He wrote about them in caustic terms, describing their vile behavior and the disastrous results of following their error. He had equally strong words for godly leaders, mandating that they stand up for right doctrine. Part of Peter's legacy was confronting lies and protecting his followers from error. It was so important that he included it as part of his timeless instructions for leaders.

By the time Peter wrote his second letter, some wicked people had wormed their way into church leadership. He revealed them as "false prophets" and "false teachers" who "secretly bring in destructive heresies." They had gone so far as to deny "the Master who bought them" with the result being "the way of truth will be blasphemed." Peter called them "arrogant people" who "do not tremble when they blaspheme the glorious ones." He likened them to "irrational animals" who "speak blasphemies about things they don't understand." These false teachers demonstrated dubious morality. They "consider it a pleasure to carouse in the daytime . . . delighting in their deceptions" with "eyes full of adultery . . . always looking for sin." Further, these leaders "seduce unstable people and have hearts trained in greed."

These false teachers were "springs without water, mists driven by a whirlwind" casting a "gloom of darkness" and by "uttering boastful, empty words, they seduce, with fleshly desires and debauchery." They were "slaves of corruption" and cursed because they had "escaped the world's impurity through the knowledge of our Lord and Savior Jesus Christ" but wound up "entangled in these things and defeated, the last state . . . worse . . . than the first."

As part of this pretense-stripping description, Peter also promised a violent end for these false teachers. He promised swift destruction because "their condemnation, pronounced long ago, is not idle, and their destruction does not sleep." Peter then used a series of biblical illustrations about the sureness of God's judgment—the angels who rebelled against God before creation, wicked men in Noah's time, inhabitants of Sodom and Gomorrah—to make his point. In contrast to this false teaching, Peter reminded his followers that a donkey once spoke a word from God and judgment followed those who rejected the message. Peter culminated his description of these vile heretics by observing that "a dog returns to its own vomit" and "a sow, after washing itself, wallows in the mud."

Peter blistered false teachers. He minced no words in describing their heresy and its outcome. He compared them to the most despicable villains in the past—cosmic and human rebels responsible for misery, suffering, and destruction. Confronting these leaders was serious business, and Peter made sure unmasking them was part of his legacy. Standing strong in the face of false teachers inside and outside the church may be part of your leadership legacy as well.

Most leaders, reading Peter's instructions, probably imagine confronting false teachers through preaching, teaching, and writing. These are viable means to point out error. When a false teacher takes a public stand, however, open rebuke is biblically appropriate. Those of us who have public leadership responsibilities know public analysis, evaluation, and critique comes with the territory. False teachers may be confronted through the same media they use to promulgate error.

While this is certainly one application of Peter's legacy-warning, it isn't the only application. You may not, for example, be a leader with a communication platform. You don't preach, teach, or write—and if you do, only a small number of people may be aware of your work. There are, however, other venues for confronting false teaching and its results. This might be described as personal apologetics—the process of correcting false teaching (the results of false teachers) more than correcting the teachers themselves.

Some of my best personal apologetics, for example, was done while parenting. My children were exposed to false teachers and teachings through television, public education, and their friends. No matter how cloistered parents keep their children, influences contradicting Christian values are inevitable. Our strategy, rather than trying to completely shield our children from these influences, was to take them on aggressively. This meant we discussed television shows, evaluated textbooks, critiqued positions taken by teachers, and dialogued (constantly, it seemed) about the opinions our children were forming from what their friends told them. These conversations went on for about twenty years.

Rather than lecture our children (which, like all parents, we did sometimes), our primary goal and methodology was honest dialogue. The subjects ran the gamut from church participation to gambling to going to strip clubs to fighting in wars to caring for the environment to the social impact of missionaries to political parties to drinking alcohol to dating, and on and on. This was often a messy, frustrating process. When our children were younger, the dialogue was structured in the context of requiring obedience. As they moved through their teen years, however, we moved away from demanding obedience to laying out options and consequences. Often our children made good choices, but sometimes they didn't. In those cases, it was hard to watch them struggle with the consequences. Apologist parents present the Bible's standards and expectations frankly, but realize that freedom to choose means some lousy choices will be made along the way. Some of our hardest conversations ended this way, "You know what we believe is right. We think, in the long run, you will be better off if you follow biblical principles. You decide, but either way, the consequences are yours."

Confronting false teachers doesn't always mean preaching a sermon, writing a blog, publishing a book, or teaching a seminar. Sometimes your toughest apologetics will be done over coffee with a friend who is contemplating having an affair, with a young person considering an abortion, or an employee making questionable financial decisions. These are real-life situations and decisions are made based on what someone else has told them is acceptable behavior. Your task is presenting the truth of Scripture and confronting the false ideas derived from false teaching. Be careful at this point. Personal apologetics isn't about attacking the confused person sitting across from you. Their thoughts are the result of false teachers or errant teaching. They are not the source of the falsehood. Remembering this distinction will increase your patience, lessen your anger, and generate conversations rather than lectures. Attacking a confused person who has been victimized by false information won't change their mind. Keep your focus on the real problem (misinformation that contradicts Scripture) and the ultimate goal (changed choices based on biblical principles).

When our children had cockamamie ideas, we knew they came from some false teaching source they had encountered in the culture. Confronting those ideas with better ideas was more important than getting into an argument. In an objective dialogue, Christian ethics are always the most winsome option. Confusion, rooted in what sin has done to our reasoning capacity, means the right choices won't always be made. Nonetheless, communicating truth in love even while confronting falsehood is still your responsibility. Doing it well requires spiritual conviction and verbal dexterity. Taking courses or reading books on biblical interpretation, theology, ethics, and apologetics is helpful. Remember, though: your objective isn't to beat up people with information. Your task is telling them the truth, as lovingly and patiently as possible, and confronting the false teaching rather than attacking the person who has been duped by it.

Standing up to false teachers and false teaching can take many forms. Stand strong to the end of your life. Be as kind as possible but don't shy away from holding firm on biblical standards—both in public comments and personal appeals. Doing this well extends those standards, through the lives of people you influence, to the next generation.

QUESTIONS FOR REFLECTION

1. Why is confronting false teachers difficult? How can you gain more courage for this responsibility?
2. What does it mean to confront false teaching rather than attack the person duped into believing it? How can you improve in this area?
3. How can you improve as a personal apologist?
4. How can you communicate this conviction as part of your leadership legacy?
5. Which of Peter's leadership priorities might have helped form this part of his legacy?

Conviction 9

ANTICIPATE THE LORD'S RETURN

2 Peter 3:1–13

 If you have been a leader long enough to think about leaving a legacy, you have learned that life isn't fair, that people are sometimes dishonest, that circumstances can be trying, and—no matter how hard you work—that results can be disappointing. It might seem like Peter, of all people, would have had a different experience. He didn't. Some Christians read the Bible with rose-colored glasses, romanticizing first-century leaders and wrongly assuming their life experiences were a continued series of successes. Peter had some significant accomplishments, to be sure, but he also went through some very trying situations. The stories in Acts alone prove this point.

Living through negative leadership situations and grappling with disappointing results can be draining. After a while, you just want to give up. You get tired of dealing with people, slogging through the battle day after day, and struggling to keep up. Resources—spiritual, human, and financial—are limited, and it's hard to press on when progress seems hopeless. You long for justice and righteousness to triumph, but really, you would settle for just a little more fairness. Some of my worst times as a leader have been the lonely days when immoral, unethical, or abusive people prevailed. One particular day, after months of grueling legal and political wrangling on a multimillion-dollar problem, our ministry experienced a major defeat. I met with our team and told them, "Today, we lost—and we lost big. It wasn't just a setback, it was a whipping. Evil won today, and we have to come back tomorrow and figure out what to do next." That was a bad day.

What sustains leaders through times like this? What part of Peter's written legacy relates to solving this dilemma? What did he learn and what did he want to pass down to us that can keep us going when it appears that evil has the upper hand? The answer: Jesus is coming, and he will make everything right in the end.

Peter felt so strongly about this part of his legacy that he mentioned it in both his letters. He also tied this part of his second letter to the previous section about false teachers by writing, "Scoffers will come in the last days to scoff . . . saying, 'Where is the promise of His coming?'" Peter acknowledged the seeming slowness of Jesus' return. Many first-century believers assumed his promised return would happen relatively quickly. Already because of the supposed delay, some were questioning the legitimacy of expecting Jesus to return. Peter reminded his followers, "ever since the fathers fell asleep, all things continue as they have been since the beginning of creation." God's timing of future events extends longer than might be expected from a human perspective.

Peter made the point even more plainly, writing, "don't let this one thing escape you: With the Lord one day is like a thousand years, and a thousand years like one day." He also underscored that God's timetable is his alone since "the Lord does not delay His promise, as some understand delay." Some people were apparently trying to predict the Lord's return based on circumstantial evidence or their interpretation of the signs of the times. Peter confounded this with the illustration, "the Day of the Lord will come like a thief," meaning no one can predict when Jesus will return. He will come unexpectedly, when many are unprepared or unaware, making his appearance in his time and his way.

The Lord's return will culminate human history. It will bring ultimate judgment and make all things right. This aspect of Jesus' return gives hope. When Jesus returns, everything temporal will be destroyed—from the heavens to the earth to the human authorities in between. When Jesus returns and God's judgment is over, we will experience "the new heavens and a new earth, where righteousness will dwell." The ultimate rule and reign of Jesus, bringing justice to every unfair situation and correcting every dastardly wrong endured by his people, is our enduring hope. It's what keeps us going through the evil, entangling quagmire of ministry leadership in a broken world.

The longer you lead, the more susceptible you become to discouragement, cynicism, and bitterness. Frankly, losing hurts. It's painful when evil prevails. No matter how hard you preach, teach, and counsel, people still make horrible choices that destroy relationships, families, and churches. No matter how carefully you strategize, sinful people will undermine your best efforts. Political systems, governing authorities, and corporate practices all bear the taint of sin and seem to conspire against spiritual progress. When these forces align, it's tough to maintain faith. When a ministry organization loses money or people or influence because of unjust practices, it's easy to just give up. Why try when the deck seems stacked against us?

You must maintain faith in God's promises and strive for the best, believing that God's ways will produce positive results. The only problem is, sometimes they don't. That admission may shock you. As a Christian leader, you might expect me to claim otherwise. The fact is, God's people are sometimes thwarted, not just in their lifetimes but for several generations. Remember four hundred years of slavery in Egypt? Spiritual forces, evil people, and imperfect institutions conspire to produce this grim reality.

Hope is only lost when our perspective is skewed. God promises to make all things right at the end of time, not at the end of your project, ministry career, or lifetime. Justice is coming. God's ways will prevail. God's work will be established. Righteousness will reign. Every unfair outcome will be reversed. Every abused Christian will be justified. Peter's legacy letter reminds us that Jesus is coming—then, and only then, will all things be made right. Not before, not necessarily in your lifetime, and certainly not on your timetable.

Part of your leadership legacy is maintaining hope to the end of your life. Doing so isn't simply practicing a high level of spiritual denial. Hope takes the pains and problems of the world seriously, admitting the worst of them. Hope also admits, in the short run, that God's people may be abused and his work stymied. Hope begins with honesty about life as it is, not as we wish it would be. Hope, however, isn't overwhelmed by these immediate realities.

Hope results from a fixation on the future return of Jesus Christ. It may seem like a far distant reality, but it's nonetheless the ultimate reality.

Jesus promised he will return. When he appears, he promises the world will be remade without the curse of sin. Christians will finally celebrate life, service, and worship without the taint of sin. Finally and forever, God's work and God's ways will prevail. All injustice will be rectified, all relationships restored, all motives purified, and all situations resolved fairly. Every wrong will be righted. Think about that the next time you are on the losing end of a leadership challenge, abused by some unethical politician, cheated by an unscrupulous businessman, or undermined by an unregenerate church member. Your losses are temporary—real and painful, yes. But still only temporary.

Without confidence in Jesus' return, your leadership legacy may degenerate as you become bitter and cynical. Part of your legacy is finishing strong, keeping your faith in the possibilities of God's people accomplishing ministry. Another significant aspect of legacy is to encourage younger leaders to press ahead, even when you know they won't always be successful. You can't fake motivation for these legacy-leaving contributions. You will stay strong to the extent that your hope is settled on something beyond your lifetime of experiences fraught with failure. Your hope must be fixed on this eternal reality: Jesus is coming soon, and when he does, all things will be made right. Let that stirring affirmation guide and motivate the legacy you leave. Despite the likelihood of mixed results now, it's worth leading because Jesus is coming again.

QUESTIONS FOR REFLECTION

1. How often do you think about the return of Jesus? Why don't you think of it more often?
2. What injustice are you facing or have you faced that hasn't yet been rectified? How will you trust Jesus to make things right in the future?
3. How does your concept of hope change when you link it to the second coming of Jesus?
4. How can you communicate this conviction as part of your leadership legacy?
5. Which of Peter's leadership priorities might have helped form this part of his legacy?

Conviction 10

GIVE GLORY TO JESUS

2 Peter 3:14–18

 Peter closed his second letter, the final words of his written legacy, with a stirring crescendo. His final thoughts are the culmination of all he intended to communicate and magnify as his ultimate message—that we should give glory to Jesus. When a Christian leader comes to the end of a long and fruitful life, the ultimate goal is to magnify the Lord. Our legacy isn't so much what we have done or convictions we have modeled. It's Jesus—his life, his work through us, and the good done by his grace.

Some parts of Peter's written legacy were stern, harsh-sounding warnings and rebukes. When he got to the end, however, his tone changed. He addressed his recipients twice as "dear friends," emphasizing his affection for and fellowship with them. His previously written blunt words were for their benefit, confronting problems that would trip them up and minimize their faithfulness to Jesus. Peter's goal was to build up, not tear down, even when he was stridently condemning false teachers and issuing other warnings. Legacy-leavers are like that. While we don't shy away from tackling tough issues or holding controversial positions, our ultimate goal is to make a lasting positive contribution, not leave perpetual controversy.

Peter also concluded his legacy with kind words about Paul, equating his writings with Scripture. He confessed that some of Paul's "letters . . . are hard to understand." That's comforting in a humorous way. It's good to know that Paul has always been complicated. Peter and Paul had an interesting relationship—a partnership in some instances (Acts 15) and open conflict in others (Gal. 2). The last words from Peter about Paul acknowledge the complexity of Paul's ministry, but also affirm it and commend it to the church for all time. Legacy-leavers speak well of other leaders; they find the good in what others have done, and they promote it for the well-being of the church.

Peter then ended his letter with another brief warning about spiritual deception. He cautioned, "be on your guard, so that you are not led away by the error of lawless people and fall from your own stability." Then, in a more positive way, he counseled, "grow in the grace and knowledge of our Lord and Savior Jesus Christ." Peter wanted his last instructions to be both positive in tone and focused in nature. His legacy wasn't primarily about confronting error or evil. It was more about pointing people to Jesus. Peter concluded with a doxology in the form of a written prayer, exclaiming, "To Him be the glory both now and to the day of eternity. Amen." At the end of Peter's life, magnifying Jesus was his ultimate legacy.

As you move through the seasons of leadership, you will likely become less and less enamored with your own accomplishments and more and more convinced of Jesus' supremacy. My early leadership years were spent trying to prove myself—to make a mark. My motives were mixed, more pure some days than others, but still a jumbled mess of spiritual motivation (doing God's will) and my perspiration (making a name for myself). An interesting change has happened along the way. I have become more and more aware of my inadequacies, and less convinced that my leadership skills are the source of my lasting legacy. Many days, my leadership challenges overwhelm me. I don't have the wisdom, insight, intelligence, or passion to be successful. I'm increasingly aware that much of my leadership has really involved just showing up and experiencing circumstances only God can orchestrate or control.

While I'm currently in the leading phase, my legacy season is rapidly approaching. Every day, more of my life is in the rearview mirror. I'm starting to think about what I will leave behind. More and more, my accomplishments wane in comparison to the things Jesus does through me and around me. For example, writing this book is a nice accomplishment. Looking at Peter's life as an example of the seasons of a leader's life has been a labor of love for me. I have learned new insights during the process and have become a better leader through this study. My hope is that it will encourage many and inspire some toward the same end. If you have read this far, it has probably helped you in some way.

While working on this book, however, I helped a man commit his life to Jesus as Savior and Lord. Like a midwife, I was in the room when he was born again—catching the baby, so to speak. My part was minimal as Jesus saved him, changing him in an instant from a deluded, new-age religionist to a new person in Christ. Over the past year, I have been coaching him through his early discipleship, helping him grow in his newfound faith. The transformation has been incredible and beyond anything I can take credit for causing. Watching Jesus remake a man—initially through conversion and then gradually through sanctification—has been breathtaking and humbling. No mistake about it, Jesus has done this miracle without much help from me. Watching it has been an awe-inspiring reminder of how powerful Jesus is, and how unable I am to do anything truly significant on my own. The information in a thousand books can't do what Jesus did in a nanosecond—change a man's nature.

My legacy, like yours, has many dimensions. You may leave behind a church or ministry, a company or community that's better because of your influence. You may leave behind children and grandchildren whose lives are enriched by following your example, adopting your convictions, and practicing wisdom passed down to them. You may set athletic records, carve a beautiful statue, build thousands of houses, or leave a lot of money to a good cause. You may even write your legacy, distilling your convictions—like Peter—into short letters or long books summarizing key insights you have learned over a lifetime of experiencing God.

When you get to the end, however, will all of it combined even come close to what Jesus has accomplished in and through you? Not hardly! Your ultimate legacy is giving glory to Jesus for what he has done in your life, praising him for what he's accomplished despite your inadequacies, and thanking him for enabling you to leave behind a blessing for others. When it's all said and done, let the last word in your legacy be "Jesus." Your legacy is more about him and what he has done through you than it is about you and what you have done for him. Like Peter, may your legacy be the story of how you were able to "grow in the grace and knowledge of our Lord and Savior Jesus Christ. To Him be the glory both now and to the day of eternity. Amen."

QUESTIONS FOR REFLECTION

1. As your life has unfolded, how has Jesus become more prominent in your leadership?
2. What are some things Jesus has done through you or for you that are central to your legacy?
3. How can you bring more attention to Jesus in the legacy you are leaving?
4. How can you communicate this conviction as part of your leadership legacy?
5. Which of Peter's leadership priorities might have helped form this part of his legacy?